C000121726

MONTY
A LIFE IN PHOTOGRAPHS
1887 - 1976

MONTY
A LIFE IN PHOTOGRAPHS

THE FAMILY, LIFE AND TIMES OF FIELD MARSHAL THE VISCOUNT MONTGOMERY OF ALAMEIN
—————— 1887 - 1976 ——————

Brian Montgomery

BLANDFORD PRESS
POOLE · DORSET

First published in the UK 1985 by Blandford Press
Link House, West Street, Poole, Dorset, BH15 1LL

Text copyright © 1985 Brian Montgomery

Distributed in the United States by
Sterling Publishing Co., Inc.,
2 Park Avenue, New York, NY 10016

British Library Cataloguing in Publication Data

Montgomery, Brian
    Monty : a life in photographs : the family and times
    of Field Marshall the Viscount Montgomery of
    Alamein, KG, GCB, DSO, LLD, DL, 1887-1976.
    1. Montgomery of Alamein, Bernard Law Montgomery,
    Viscount   2. Great Britain.
    Army—Biography
    3. Generals—Great Britain—Biography
    355.3′31′0924   DA69.3.M56

ISBN 0 7137 1494 8

All rights reserved. No part of this book may be reproduced
or transmitted in any form or by any means, electronic or
mechanical, including photocopying, recording or any
information storage and retrieval system, without permission
in writing from the publisher.

Typeset by August Filmsetting, Haydock, St. Helens
Printed in Great Britain
by Hazell, Watson, and Viney, Aylesbury

Other books by Brian Montgomery
A Field Marshal In the Family
Monty's Grandfather – A Life's Service to the Raj
Shenton of Singapore – Governor and Prisoner of War

DEDICATED TO ALL THOSE WHO
SERVED UNDER MONTY'S COMMAND

CONTENTS

Early in 1983, my wife Bunty had suggested that we should write this book, and she did in fact see and approve its synopsis; thus leaving my stepson Tom MacNeece, with his professional eyes, to oversee the writing of the whole work and urge its completion. I am therefore doubly grateful to him for his wise counsel and advice at every stage of the task.

I have been most fortunate in having so many family members to turn to for help, and not only in providing illustrations to supplement the large number of photographs Monty had left me, but also for the advantage of factual information, which they drew from their memories and generously passed on to me. In these terms, I am particularly grateful to my sister Lady Michelmore and my sister-in-law Margaret Montgomery, and for the absolute support of my nephew and his wife Viscount and Viscountess Montgomery of Alamein. My nephew Gardner Montgomery, now resident in the USA, provided the illustration of Monty's great-great-grandfather, Samuel Montgomery, who was a wine and spirits merchant in Londonderry. I am equally grateful to Monty's two stepsons and their wives, John and Jocelyn Carver, with Dick and (the late) Audrey Carver.

I have much reason to be grateful to the other family members cited below who, by the quality of their information and the support they gave me (in consultation, correspondence, or comment) contributed so much to the scope of the illustrations and their linking text. My cousin Canon John Darlington provided contemporary photographs of St Mark's Vicarage and its garden at Kennington Oval; and I was fortunate indeed in having the generous co-operation and friendship of several of Dean Farrar's great-grandchildren – all descended from the Dean's daughter, Evelyn Thomas. Sally and David Mure gave me invaluable access to Honor Thomas's two volumes of family photographs, which covered five generations of her family. I should add that this book could not have been completed without the ever ready help and support of Sally Mure and it was Sarah Mure who took, and sent to me from Tasmania, photographs of Bishopscourt in Hobart, where Monty spent his early boyhood. My thanks are also due to Jack and Imogen Thomas for their hospitality, and the insight they gave me into their family history, including the significance of Haileybury in our Montgomery background. I am grateful for the advice and comments I received from Mary and Roger Kingsley, and Grizelda and Spencer Maurice. It was Nicholas Thomas who, just in time, provided for illustration what is probably the only likeness in existence of Mrs Frederic Farrar, Dean Farrar's wife née Lucy Mary Cardew.

I owe a deep debt of gratitude to Sir Denis and Lady Hamilton for all the time and trouble they have taken to help me with the writing of this work; in this same context I must add Francis and Peggy Powell-Brett, who were always so tolerant of my frequent calls for advice or information.

My research involved personal contact with, and requests for assistance from, a number of sources, and I am sincerely grateful to the following individuals for their very generous assistance.

Sheena Barber, Peter Burrin, the Reverend Sir Nicholas Rivett-Carnac, Air Chief Marshal Sir Hugh Constantine, Peter Earle, Greta Gynt, Sir Tom Hopkinson, Garnett Kempson, Harry Lade (Australia), Hanna Longrigg, Lady McIndoe, Elizabeth Macdonald, Dr T.K. Maurice, the late Oscar Nemon, Barbara Pearson, Raymond Snowden, the Earl of Snowdon, the Rt Reverend H.A. Jerrim, Bishop of Tasmania, and the Reverend Derek Watson.

I relied much for both information and photographs on members of the following institutions, and am very conscious of their unfailing help, particularly their prompt and kind action in locating and supplying material to which I had requested access. Director Dr Alan Borg, Robert Crawford, Dr Dowling, Roderick Suddaby, Jane Carmichael and the staff of the Imperial War Museum: Peter Burrin of the Pictures Section, Central Office of Information; Major General Richard Keighley, Commandant of the Royal Military Academy Sandhurst, with his librarian J.W. Hunt and his deputy librarian M.G.H. Wright; Major A.H. Haycock, Regimental Secretary, the Royal Warwickshire Regiment and his assistant Mr A. Buckingham; Mr A. Hawkyard, Archivist at Harrow School; Mrs E.M. Denton, Archivist at St Paul's School; Mr J.D. Lee, Mr R. Bright, Roger Wemyss-Brooks and Marjorie Willis of the BBC Hulton Picture Library; Miss Oakley, Keeper of Library and Records Canterbury Cathedral; Mr A. Reedie, Curator of Canterbury Museum; the Commandant and staff of the Pakistan Command and Staff College, Quetta.

I shall always be grateful to the staff in all departments of my publishers, particularly Stuart Booth, Mildred Tyson and John Douet, for their care and guidance of my work, and their toleration of my endless queries. This book could certainly not have appeared but for the hard work, skill and patience of my secretary Susan Cowley. I was again fortunate in having Ann Hoffmann as the skilful and experienced indexer.

Finally, none of the sources which I have listed are responsible for any error of fact, interpretation, or omission which may remain, and for which I am responsible.

B.M.

I first met the C-in-C Allied Ground Forces when training my infantry battalion for Normandy. He looked at me with searing steel-grey eyes and said: 'You're rather young, how old are you?'

I was barely 25 and thought I was to be demoted – until he smiled and remarked: 'Good, I like my C.Os to be young.'

Thereafter, I served in 21 Army Group under Monty throughout the battle of Normandy and North-West Europe campaign to the liberation of Holland and the occupation of Germany. Operating from his advanced Tactical Headquarters, he made it his business to know the units under his command down to battalion level. He knew the names of every battalion C.O. and second-in-command. His professionalism was the standard to which we all aspired and his sometimes boastful ego reflected our own sense of invincible self-confidence. What a contrast to the chaos and confusion of Dunkirk, which I had experienced only a few years before! To be sure, we had better equipment, air support, tanks and, above all, new allies; but the effect Monty had on morale, his example of crusading zeal, his absolute dedication to the job, and his determination to spread his military gospel to the million or so troops under his command: I doubt whether, in the history of the world, we will ever see another General of his kind.

I was proud to serve under Monty, and I am proud to have been asked to write this foreword to Brian Montgomery's book recording Monty's life in photographs. His *A Field Marshal in the Family* published in 1973, deepened our understanding of Monty's character and achievement by giving an unforgettable portrait of Monty's forefathers and family background. This volume of photographs will provide a remarkable companion – a further memorial to the greatest British field commander in modern times.

SIR DENIS HAMILTON,
DSO, TD

PHOTOGRAPHIC CREDITS

Many of the photographs in this book are from private
collections, family albums and other individual sources. Kind
permission for their use is very gratefully acknowledged.

The nature and age of some photographs included has
meant that it has proved impossible to trace their original
source, or copyright owner. Whilst every effort has been made
to trace and acknowledge these origins, it is hoped and
requested in sincerity that the ultimate owners of any
photograph which may have been inadvertently uncredited,
or erroneously credited, will accept apologies in the spirit and
nature of their choice and use – in order to illustrate and
honour a great man, his life and his times.

Many 'official' photographs of Bernard Montgomery were
issued from a number of British Government and other
occasional sources over the years, especially during and
immediately following the Second World War. Most of these,
together with earlier photographs of his Army career in and
after the First World War, have become ultimately part of the
archives of the Imperial War Museum. The museum, together
with the Central Office of Information, is gratefully
acknowledged and thanked for assistance and kind permission
to use such photographs.

In addition, the following individuals and organisations are
thanked, in alphabetical order, for their help and use of
photographs on listed pages: BBC Hulton Picture Library (94,
97, 98, 124, 125, 126, 127, 128, 137, 153), John Carver OBE
(27), Air Chief Marshal Sir Kenneth Cross KCB, CBE, DSO, FC
(105), Sir Denis and Lady Hamilton (128, 138, 146), Country
Life magazine (119), Greta Gynt (121), Indian Army Staff
College, Quetta (70), Keystone Press Agency (110, 156), Press
Association with kind permission (139, 140, 157), Paul
Popper Ltd with kind permission (136, 148), Royal
Warwickshire Regiment Antelope magazine (65, 66, 67, 68,
69), Sandhurst Library (44), Shaw Savill Line (28), Lord
Snowdon (145), Thomson Organisation with kind permission
(142), Times Newspapers with kind permission (125, 129,
130, 131, 133, 148), Westminster School Pauline magazine
(96).

'WHAT PEACEFUL HOURS I ONCE ENJOYED!
HOW SWEET THEIR MEMORY STILL!'

William Cowper: (Olney Hymns I)

These words are surely true, particularly when memories are provoked by the sight of old photographs in family albums, or on seeing the haphazard evidence in snapshots taken by relatives or friends on various social occasions. Those memories are stirred all the more when such photographs are accompanied sometimes by amateur drawings, pictures or postcards of people and events, nearly always with at least a brief caption to show place and date (even if only the year) and the identity of the people portrayed.

Family records like these have been kept since the early days of photography, which generally means the appearance of the portrait lens in 1841 and, by and large, the larger the family the greater the size of the collection.

In this volume, compiled from old family photographs and other contemporary illustrations, I have tried to draw the life story, chiefly in chronological sequence from birth to death, of a great British soldier; Field Marshal the Viscount Montgomery of Alamein KG, GCB, DSO, LLD, DL, who became known almost world wide as 'Monty'.

The problem has been to present Monty not merely as a military commander, for that has been well done so often, but in his very widest sense, which was that of a phenomenon. For Monty became truly a part of the social, political, and military history of Britain, just as much as Wellington, Nelson, Kitchener and Roberts were in their day, and during times equally fraught with uncertainty and grave dangers. That has been my task; to make this vision of him shine through the pictures, and with the minimum of page print.

So many photographs of my brother have been produced, as well as drawings, cartoons, likenesses in one form or another (fair and unfair, good and bad) that there must be scores of thousands in all the developed countries of the world. But I have a very large number of pictures of Monty in my personal possession, or available from my family and other sources. Thus I have tried to avoid using previously published pictures unless entirely necessary.

My story begins with the record of our family history, its origins and social background, in order to show how the influence of heredity and environment played such a large part in shaping the character, attitudes, actions and opinions of this great man.

BRIAN MONTGOMERY
Chelsea, London
March, 1985

The first person with the surname Montgomery to appear in Great Britain was Sir Roger de Montgomeri. He was a Norman, a distinguished and successful soldier, and one of the most powerful and influential nobles at the Court of William, Duke of Normandy, later William I King of England, and whose kinsman he was. Sir Roger's family had owned large estates in the region of Caen, Falaise and Argentan – the very area in which, in the summer of 1944, Field Marshal Montgomery trapped and destroyed the German armies under Field Marshal Rommel. Roger had commanded the vanguard of the Norman army at the Battle of Hastings in 1066, and also contributed sixty ships to Duke William's fleet.

After the Norman Conquest, Roger Montgomeri was rewarded by William I with honours and much property on the Welsh border, where he built the castle at Shrewsbury and gave his name to the town and county of Montgomery. From his line were descended all the numerous Montgomery families of England, Wales, Scotland and Ireland, whether their name is spelt Montgomerie, as in Scotland, or Montgomery elsewhere. Centuries later came the Protestant plantation of the nine counties of Ulster, begun by King James I of England about 1609. This brought into Ireland, generally from Scotland, all the many and subsequently Irish Montgomery families. Included were our family branch in Co. Donegal, probably in the seventeenth century during the reign of King Charles II. However, all we know for certain is that our own branch was settled at Killaghtee in south-west Donegal by 1700, and became part of the new breed, the Protestant Anglo-Irish, who possessed all the typical Irish intelligence and keen sense of humour, backed by Scots logic and industry.

Before 1750, young Samuel Montgomery, aged twenty-four, left Killaghtee and established a wholesale and retail wine and spirits business in Londonderry. He lived in the city but prospered exceedingly and soon bought from the Marquis of Donegal some one thousand acres of farm and hill land in Inishowen, that wild and remote region of mountains, moors, bog and rough pasture that lies between Lough Foyle and Lough Swilly. But Samuel loved this far northern part of Co. Donegal. He sensed its real beauty and built our family home there, which he called New Park, on ground where now stands the small town of Moville. He had first married a local girl who became the great-great-grandmother of the Field-Marshal.

Our great-great-grandfather Samuel Montgomery (1726–1803). He was a wine merchant who eventually became Chamberlain of Derry City.

This photograph is taken from an old family miniature it shows Samuel in his 18th century dress clothes around 1750, the year in which he married Anne, daughter of Marino Porter, who was the surveyor of Greencastle at the mouth of Lough Foyle, and his wife Mary Cary. In those far off times there was no established customs and excise service, and the whole population of Inishowen were mainly occupied in illicit trade, particularly the distillation and marketing of home brewed whisky, or potheen. Presumably Samuel's sale of spirits in Derry prospered accordingly!

W S M
1931

New Park, Moville, Co. Donegal, our family home completed by Samuel Montgomery in 1773. It was built of local grey stone with three storeys, and had ten bedrooms.

Bedrooms were very necessary as the Montgomery wives bred prolifically, in the custom of the eighteenth and nineteenth centuries. Samuel had eight children, whilst his eldest son's wife had her last baby (a son) when she was fifty-three! Sir Robert Montgomery followed with eight children and Bishop Montgomery had nine. New Park did not have the architectural beauty generally associated with Georgian country houses, but the main windows had bow-fronts, and inside the rooms were spacious, with a wide hall and a shallow curving staircase to upper floors. Samuel planned his home well, with a wide terrace, large garden, and a demesne of sixty acres, all on the western shore of Lough Foyle and running up into the Donegal Hills. A later generation built an open air squash racquets court where the children of each generation played endlessly; there the Field Marshal began to learn his skill at tennis and develop his eye for all ball games. New Park is now a hotel.

Our Great-grandfather The Rev. Samuel Law Montgomery (1768–1832), eldest son of Samuel who built New Park.

Samuel Law, the Field Marshal's great-grandfather, was evidently a very different person from Samuel, the wine merchant. A somewhat solemn character, he was fervently religious and educated at Foyle College, Londonderry, from where he graduated at Trinity College, Dublin, before being ordained in the Protestant Church of Ireland. He was Rector of Moville, his home parish, for many years until he died there in 1832. His wife was an Irish girl from Trintaugh in Co. Donegal, née Susan McClintock, whom he married in the year when his father died. His six children, three sons and three daughters, were all born at New Park; it was Susan, his wife, who had her last baby at the age of fifty-three. Her second son, who became Sir Robert Montgomery, spent his early years and childhood entirely at New Park.

Sir Robert Montgomery (1809–1887).

This photograph is the earliest known picture of our distinguished grandfather Sir Robert Montgomery, GCSI, KCB, LD. It shows him as he was in 1843, at the age of thirty-four, when on three years' furlough from Allahabad in India, in the service of the East India Company.

Robert was an Ulsterman born and bred. Educated at Foyle College and the East India Company's Military College at Addiscombe, he joined the Company's Civil Service, not its armies. He always led a very active outdoor physical life, constantly on horseback in the fashion of his time. He was only nineteen when in 1828 he disembarked at Calcutta, on his first appointment as Assistant Magistrate and Collector at Azamgarh, a very remote and desolate district in what is now Uttar Pradesh. There he came under the influence of Mr James Thomason, his superior officer, who was not only a most able administrator but also a fanatical churchman and a strict member of the Evangelical party. Thomason was to play a major part in the dramatic events leading up to the Sepoy Mutiny in India in 1857.

James Thomason, taken from a painting of about 1843 and showing him as a provincial governor in India, aged about 40. Note his trousers, strapped under the boot for riding and which men generally wore daily before the coming of jodhpurs.

Four years after Robert arrived at Azamgarh, Thomason's sister, Frances Mary, arrived to stay with her brother. She was only seventeen years old, a simple and retiring young girl with a placid nature, very pious and humble and opposed to publicity of any kind. She was slim, a brunette, and very attractive in a demure way. But she was desperately lonely and quite unable to come to terms with the very stark physical conditions of life then in India. In these circumstances (there were only four white people at Azamgarh) Robert Montgomery and Frances Thomason were married in 1834. However, she died of smallpox and was buried at Allahabad after only eight years of marriage, having borne Robert three children. Her life ended before photography came to India, and unfortunately there is no painting or other likeness of her.

Ellen Jane Montgomery, née Lambert, Robert Montgomery's second wife, aged 30, at Lahore c. 1848

After Frances Montgomery died, Robert returned to the UK for three years' furlough; he had already served fourteen years in India and this was the only time he left the subcontinent in nearly forty years.

During his furlough, Robert travelled widely and in London he met Miss Ellen Jane Lambert, the only daughter of an English family who had been settled for centuries at Woodmanstone in Surrey. She was very beautiful, with dark brown hair, a high intelligent forehead and full mouth, large grey eyes and wonderful colouring; she was fifteen years younger than Robert and, more important, no stranger to India for she was born in Bengal when her father had been a merchant in Calcutta. So they married and the two returned to India in 1846. Robert was now a senior officer and was soon appointed as Commissioner in the Punjab.

Ellen always had great influence over her husband and brought to him that breadth of view which is frequently so lacking in a Protestant Ulsterman. She was a very powerful character, full of common sense, and spent nearly twenty years in India with 'Monty' (Sir Robert was always called Monty) with only one visit to England. She died in 1919 at the age of 95, having outlived her husband by thirty-two years. No one was ever allowed to mention Sir Robert's first marriage in her presence!

The large bungalow in Lahore, in the Punjab, which Sir Robert built in 1849 and called New Park.

He and Ellen were living here long before the mutiny began, together with their eight children (of Robert's two marriages) whose ages ranged from twenty-one years to one year; this included Sir Robert's eldest son, Henry, the future Bishop Montgomery, who became Monty's father.

Very early photograph taken around 1855 at Dharmsala hill station. Sir Robert is seen holding his young son James Alexander Lawrence Montgomery (always known in our family as Uncle Jimmie) who, when he grew up, served with great distinction in the Indian Civil Service. Also sitting at the table is Robert's daughter, Frances Mary; by his first marriage. Sitting next to her is her husband Sir Donald McLeod whom she had married on her nineteenth birthday; tragically she died before she was twenty.

It was the hot weather when this picture was taken, yet Sir Robert is wearing a high black stock, notwithstanding the temperature; his daughter Frances is still wearing the farthingale (a wide spreading skirt on hoops) which preceded the crinoline.

Frances's sister Mary Montgomery also died young, just three years after the Indian Mutiny, as well as their younger brother who only lived until he was sixteen and about to go to Addiscombe. Thus all three children of Robert's first marriage died very young in life, for which his second wife was apparently not ill-pleased!

Another early photograph of Robert about 1856, the year before the Indian Mutiny began, when he was Judicial Commissioner of the Punjab and Second-in-Command to Sir John Lawrence, the Chief Commissioner of the Province. He is still wearing that high black stock!

Opposite: Montgomery Hall, erected in 1870 in memory of Sir Robert, in the Public Park at Lahore, by the People and Princes of the Punjab. Later on, and in our time, this building became the Lahore Gymkhana Club.

When Sir Robert and his wife returned to England they bought No. 7 Cornwall Gardens, the large house which stands today at the junction of the Gardens with Gloucester Road, London SW7. In fact, Robert never retired from his professional life because he was soon appointed a member of the Secretary of State's Council for India, and was working as its Deputy Chairman when he died.

The only known photograph of Sir Robert Montgomery and Sir John Lawrence, taken alone together probably at Lahore, early in 1857 before the Indian Mutiny began.

The Lawrence family (there were five brothers who served in India under the East India Company) came from Coleraine in Co. Antrim within sight of Co. Donegal. They all went to Foyle College and it was there that the Lawrence-Montgomery association began and continued during their lifetime.

This is Sir Robert Montgomery's camel carriage outside Government House, Lahore, with its accompanying retinue of six cameleers and six camels, two outriders and four or more servants; the latter travelled in a separate four-wheeled covered wagonette that conveyed the drinks and refreshments that the Lieutenant Governor should never be without! Sir Robert used this carriage extensively during his six years (1859–1865) as Lieutenant Governor of the Punjab, before he finally returned to the UK.

Three generations of our family are shown in this photograph. It was taken in the garden in front of New Park, Moville, in the summer of 1886.

Sir Robert is unmistakeable, with his wife standing behind him. His daughter, Lucy, is on the far left with her husband, the Rev. Roger Dalison beside her. Then, standing, are two of his sons, Bishop Montgomery (bearded) behind our mother, and Colonel Montgomery (Uncle Jimmie) home on leave from India. The third generation is represented by six of Sir Robert's grandchildren. The Field Marshal was not born until the following year.

Sir Robert Montgomery, from a marble bust by the sculptor Bruce Joy, that stands to this day in London in a main corridor of the Foreign and Commonwealth Office in Whitehall.

Sir Robert died at Cornwall Gardens on 28 December 1887. He lived just long enough to see his grandson, the future Field Marshal, who was born six weeks before he died. There are memorials to Sir Robert in the crypt of St Paul's Cathedral, in our family church at Moville, and at Foyle College, and in the Cathedrals of Lahore and Londonderry.

ROBERT MONTGOMERY

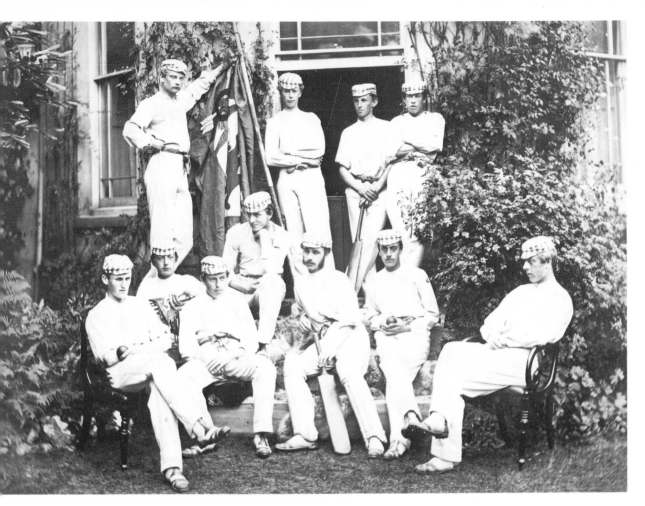

Bishop (Henry) Montgomery, standing in third row on the extreme left, taken when he was a young man at Harrow aged 18, in the 1st XI cricket team, and about to go to Trinity College, Cambridge.

He was born at Cawnpore after Sir Robert and Ellen arrived there following their marriage in England. He was famous in his day as an athlete and excelled at all games, particularly cricket and football; he also won all the school races, hurdles and flat, and the fencing prizes. There can be no doubt from where the Field Marshal inherited his skill at games and sport. Henry was very religious and never considered entering any other profession than the Church. Educated in the classical tradition he went to Cambridge, not, as he put it, 'just to play cricket', but to work and study, and graduated with an Honours Degree in the Moral Sciences Tripos. But he was very broad-minded, with a keen sense of humour, and eventually became well known as a Bishop of the Anglican church and famous throughout the world, being Secretary of the Society for the Propagation of the Gospel, Prebendary of St Paul's Cathedral and, for twenty-eight years, Prelate of the Order of St Michael and St George.

Henry Montgomery in 1865 as Captain of Harrow 1st XI Football; the team won all their matches.

The Rt Rev. Bishop
Montgomery, KCMG, DD, DCL,
father of Field Marshal
Montgomery.

This photograph, taken
around 1930, outside the
family church built by
Samuel Law Montgomery in
the grounds of New Park,
illustrates the eminence of
the high position in the
Church of England which the
Bishop gained in his lifetime.
He was always very cheerful
and a perpetual optimist,
highly popular wherever he
went and a much beloved
man. The Field Marshal
adored him, as we all did,
and his influence on us was
very great.

Maud Montgomery aged 17, in about 1882, after her marriage to Henry Montgomery the previous year. She was to be the Field Marshal's mother.

She was born Maud Farrar, third daughter of Canon F.W. Farrar, who later became the Dean of Canterbury and figured largely in our family history. This drawing, by George Joy, was made as she sat for the role of *Joan of Arc*. She had first met her husband when Farrar was Rector of the parish of St Margaret's, Westminster, and Henry was one of the parish curates. The rectory was then that charming house in the south-east corner of Dean's Yard which is now the residence of Dr Rae, the Headmaster of Westminster School.

As one of the curates, Henry Montgomery was naturally a frequent visitor at the rectory, and it was not long before he became engaged to Maud. She was then only fourteen years of age and far too young to be allowed to marry her father's curate, who was thirty-one. However, they were married in the summer of 1881 by Archbishop Tait in King Henry VII's Chapel in Westminster Abbey, when she was still a young girl of sixteen. By that time Henry Montgomery had been made Vicar of the parish of St Marks, Kennington, in south London and for the next ten years (1879–1889) the young couple faced an increasingly busy life, combined with the birth of five of their nine children – six boys and three girls.

Opposite: The earliest known photograph of Field Marshal Montgomery who was born in the Vicarage of St Mark's, Kennington, on 17 November 1887.

He was one year old when this picture was taken, being then the third son and fourth child of his parents.

Canon F.W. Farrar *c.* 1876. Our maternal grandfather.

For thirteen years or so after 1876, there is no doubt that our parents were greatly influenced by Sir Robert and Lady Montgomery, at 7 Cornwall Gardens, and Canon and Mrs Farrar at Dean's Yard. Farrar, by then also Archdeacon of Westminster and Chaplain to the House of Commons, was already famous as a man of letters, a distinguished author, scholar and philologist, with a passion for the need of education as the primary occupation of young people. Farrar in particular had extensive influence over our mother and the way in which, in his view, she ought to bring up and educate her (eventually) nine children. This showed very clearly in its effect on her fourth child – Bernard, the future Field Marshal.

Miss Lucy Farrar, as a young girl aged fourteen, about 1855 and before her marriage to Dean Farrar. She was the daughter of Mr Frederick Cardew, a judge of the East India Company's Civil Service. The Cardews were an old family, long settled at Truro in Cornwall.

Our maternal grandmother, Lucy Mary Farrar, was a young and lovely girl of nineteen when, in 1860, she married the Rev. Frederic Farrar, then a master at Harrow School, where he taught for sixteen years. Bent on teaching, Farrar was then transferred for six years as Master of Marlborough before going to Westminster at Dean's Yard, where he probably did his foremost literary work. His *Life of Christ* became a classic best seller and was translated into many languages including Japanese. Actors, scholars, writers and poets all gathered at his Westminster home. Celebrities such as Henry Irving, Matthew Arnold, Tennyson, Wordsworth, the Brownings, Millais, Burne-Jones, and Carlyle were frequently there and made a deep impression on Henry and Maud Montgomery. The Farrars had ten children, five sons and five daughters. They remained at Westminster for nearly twenty years.

The very Rev. Dean Farrar, DD, FRS, *c.* 1895 when he became Dean of Canterbury. Probably one of the most famous holders of that high office, he died there in 1903, and is buried in the Cathedral Cloister Garth. His influence on his children and grandchildren was very marked.

Opposite below: Photograph of Kennington Vicarage and its large garden, *c.* 1889. The Field Marshal was born in the large bedroom on the first floor overlooking the garden.

Our parents had been ten years (1879–1889) at St Mark's Vicarage in Kennington, and had been very happy there. However in 1889, just two years after Sir Robert's death, they and their five children underwent a sudden and large scale change in their whole way of life and environment. One spring morning, Canon Farrar arrived at their vicarage to tell them that the Archbishop of Canterbury proposed that Henry should be consecrated a bishop and proceed as soon as possible to Australia, where he would become Bishop of the island state of Tasmania. Our parents had never heard of Tasmania and did not wish to leave their comfortable house with its large garden.

In those far off days there was no question of refusing a preferment to higher ecclesiastical rank, or indeed any proposal by an Archbishop – so our parents had to go! And in due course they, with their five children (Sibyl, Harold, Donald, Bernard and Una) set sail in the Shaw Savill and Albion Line steamship *SS Tainui* for Hobart, capital of Tasmania, via the Cape of Good Hope, Western Australia, and Sydney.

Moville, as it was around 1881. From the time they were married our parents always went to New Park for their summer holidays and at other times whenever possible.

The Field Marshal aged two, as he began his long voyage to Tasmania in *Tainui*.

SS Tainui, 5,031 tons.

She was a really wonderful vessel – a steel four-masted steamer cum sailing barque with clipper stem, and a yacht-like hull and bowsprit which provided a big spread of canvas on the square-rigged fore and main masts. With her beautiful hull she sat the water like a seabird, and could sail at 14 knots.

Above all, *Tainui* had very comfortable first class passenger accommodation, with bathrooms and electric light, which mattered a great deal during a voyage of nearly six weeks. The single fare first class was about 50 guineas – more than a hundred years ago.

Monty's childhood years and his time at school were remarkable not least for the fact that they were spent on two opposite sides of the world. There were the years in Tasmania with the Bishop and the family, times at Canterbury, summer holidays in Ireland at New Park and schooldays at St Paul's, where he sat his Army Entrance Examination.

Bishopscourt, Hobart, the residence of the Bishop of Tasmania where Bishop Montgomery and his family lived for thirteen years: 1889–1902. The south view facing the garden as it was at the time and as it appears today.

The house was large (eventually it had to accommodate our parents and seven children) and was built of cut stone and brick finished. The architecture, with its wide covered verandah supported on slender columns, seems to reflect the Regency decoration of England, like so many of the old Tasmania houses where the first British settlers built their homes in the mid-nineteenth century. Our parents always said how lucky they were to find 'such a friendly white society' in Tasmania, composed of four main elements – Government, military, free settlers and the descendants of convicts. A feature of the island (with its mountains it totalled some 26,000 square miles) was its English appearance, due in part to its country lanes and hedgerows.

David's, the Cathedral
church of Tasmania. Built of
local stone during the first
half of the nineteenth
century, in the English
perpendicular style, the
structure had grace and
elegance.

The cathedral was the
Bishop's delight, to which he
gave unremitting service, and
where all his family, sons and
daughters, were required to
worship regularly (though
not always his children, who
preferred the constant
outdoor life, the picnics,
riding, fishing and the like).
Looking now at this
photograph of the cathedral
taken a century ago, it is easy
to appreciate the Bishop's
pleasure in his home and
church. All the timber in
each edifice was Tasmanian
oak of the kind that, in the
1950s, Tasmania presented
to Monty for construction of
the floors in his Hampshire
home in England.

Inside Bishopscourt too the
deep religious fervour of the
Bishop and his wife, imbued
with the example and
practice of Dean Farrar,
exerted great influence. The
day began, and ended, with
family prayers, just as it had
in Dean's Yard; everyone,
sons and daughters, servants
and guests included, had to
attend. Mother in particular
kept strict discipline. One day
when Monty, still a young
boy, was caught smoking a
cigarette the Bishop called
him to prayer and they both
knelt down, whilst his father
asked God's forgiveness for
his sinful act. However,
when they left the room
there was mother, waiting
with a cane, and she
promptly gave him 'six of the
best'!

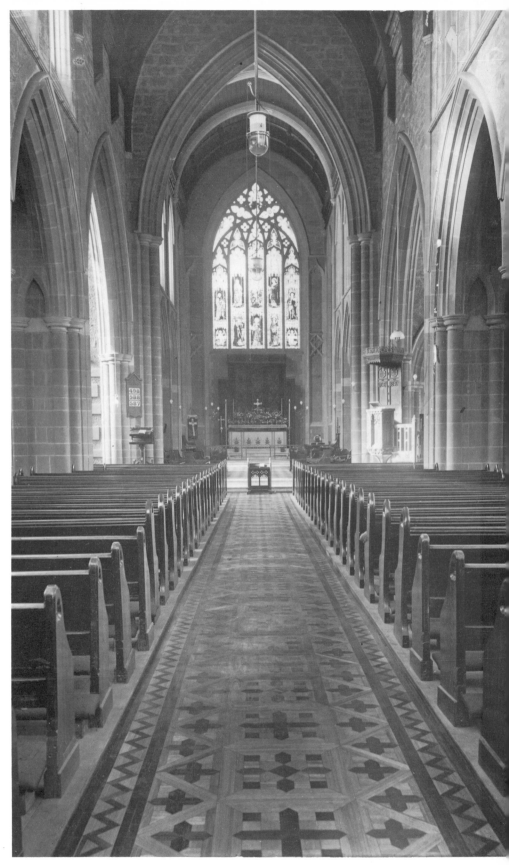

Our parents, taken one winter morning (in July) outside Bishopscourt. The Bishop had long taken to growing a moustache with a sprouting beard.

Mother was a fine horsewoman, probably at her best driving horses in harness, for she had very good (gentle) hands and drove this gig with skill and pace; she often drove tandem with ease and pleasure, displaying a gift not given to many. When driving with her husband, she always took the reins. Soon after their arrival in Hobart their life was greatly saddened by the death of their eldest child (a girl, Sybil Frances) at the early age of seven years.

Sybil Frances Montgomery, our youngest sister, with our parents in London, around 1883.

Bernard Montgomery in Tasmania aged 8 years. In those days young boys always wore Eton collars.

Monty, two years later aged 10, in Tasmania.

The 'Montgomery School' at Bishopscourt about 1900. The future Field Marshal is standing wearing a white jacket.

With her usual organising ability, our mother had arranged for tutors to come from England and take over the job of teaching her children, who were rapidly growing up, as well as children of certain close friends in Hobart or nearby. She had an extra room built on to Bishopscourt which served as a school room. The Bishop's salary was £1,000 a year, which in those times, apparently sufficed for all needs.

In the garden at Bishopscourt in 1900. This is the earliest indication of Monty's choice of the profession of arms!

A year later, 1901, aged 14
and his last year in
Tasmania.

The years the family spent
in Tasmania were
momentous for them all, both
parents and children. For the
elder children, including
Monty, it meant growing up,
the end of childhood and the
beginning of their education.
Above all, they learned to
know and understand their
parents. There is no doubt
that they all, very early in
their separate lives, grew to
appreciate the great and
wonderful man the Bishop
was. Our mother adored him
with a fierce and passionate
devotion that knew no
bounds. It was in her nature
always to be the boss, as
indeed her father Dean Farrar
would have liked to be, and it
was this that made her want
to 'wear the trousers' where
her husband was concerned,
and similarly of course to
'command' her children.
These were the factors that
led to 'troubles', sometimes,
with her children,
particularly with Monty.

Mother's difficulty was that
she had literally moved from
the school room to her
marriage, saddled with all the
manifold duties of a vicar's
life in a busy London parish,
and with her children to
bring up. Then followed,
suddenly, the translation to
the status of a diocesan
bishop's wife in a remote
British colony: yet all this
without any intervening
period. She had had neither
time nor opportunity after
leaving school to make those
close friendships with boys or
girls in her own age group,
which can be so valuable
later on. Furthermore, in
Tasmania she was so often
without her husband, for the
bishop travelled widely.

Bishop Montgomery, wearing a white helmet, on board the sailing vessel *Southern Cross* in 1892.

The Bishop chartered *Southern Cross* with her crew including fishermen, his chaplain (in front of him) and farmers, for visits to off-shore islands, including sometimes as far away as Fiji or the Solomons. Once he was away for seven months, leaving his wife and five children in Hobart.

Bishop Montgomery around 1895 and dressed for his frequent tours in the mountains and dense forests of Tasmania. But for Monty, and the whole family, great adventure was near for they were all going to visit England.

One of the happiest times in the married life of Dean and Mrs Farrar was the year 1897. For their daughter Maud and her husband Bishop Montgomery, with their large family of four boys, whose ages ranged from thirteen to one year, with two very young girls, came home from Tasmania. The Bishop had come for the Lambeth Conference of Bishops in London, and he and his family were able to make their headquarters in Canterbury.

Opposite: The Deanery in the Cathedral Close at Canterbury.

There was no room in the Deanery for so many family guests – two adults and their six children – so a large furnished, but empty, house in the Cathedral Close was taken for them, where they all spent a very happy time. The three elder boys, Harold 13, Donald 11, and Bernard (Monty) 9, all went for the summer term to the junior wing of the famous King's School, Canterbury.

The whole family spent their summer holiday at New Park; it was Monty's earliest recollection of his Irish home, before they all returned to Hobart. However, a great upheaval for the family came in 1902 when the Archbishop of Canterbury ordered the Bishop back to England as Secretary of a great missionary organisation, the Society for the Propagation of the Gospel (S.P.G.). So our parents, with their seven children, returned to London to live at 19 Bolton Road, Chiswick – a large west London suburban house and garden, that suffered bomb damage during the Second World War and has since been pulled down.

Monty, aged 16 and a schoolboy at St Paul's School, London, to which he bicycled daily from his London home.

Monty in about 1904. Croquet in the garden at New Park.

Opposite: In his last term at St Paul's.

Of the six brothers in our family, five went to St Paul's at different periods between 1902 and 1921. The sixth brother – your author – was born at Chiswick just two years after the return from Tasmania.

Brian, the ninth and youngest child of the family (late in life).

Unfortunately, notwithstanding very strong protests from Monty, the Bishop and his wife saddled this boy with the christian name initials B.F.! Brian never saw his eldest sister and scarcely saw his eldest brother, Harold, until he had grown up.

Opposite: Harold Montgomery, CMG, four years older than Monty. He was commissioned in the Imperial Yeomanry during the Boer War.

Harold was a superb horseman and essentially a practical person; very popular, highly respected and a wonderful administrator, he made Africa his life service and died in Kenya in 1958, having become Chief Native Commissioner and been awarded the CMG. He was twice married.

Montgomery

1906, at St Paul's School, Monty is now Captain of the 1st XV football team and in the cricket XI, and also a member of the school swimming VIII, of which his elder brother Donald (seated far left) is the Captain. The instructor (standing) with his swimming team was Sgt Driscoll, a famous character who coached St Paul's to victory for many years in swimming, boxing and fencing.

Monty had passed his Army entrance examination and left his public school in a blaze of athletic success. He went to Sandhurst in January 1907.

1907–1919

His Army career, so central to this story and finally so celebrated and important, started straight from school; but perhaps with less promise than history later demonstrated. In January 1907, when he was just nineteen, Monty went as a cadet to the Royal Military College, Sandhurst. His athletic record counted for much in a curriculum that consisted mainly of instruction in military subjects, particularly drill, physical training and equitation, with military history.

Rugby 1st XV at Sandhurst, Easter 1908. Monty is seated second from the right.

Equitation at Sandhurst. His riding over jumps (with his rearward seat) looks clumsy and suggests a poor performance on that occasion. Of course, this photograph was taken long before the adoption of the forward seat.

By now, it is probably well known that Monty was nearly sacked at Sandhurst. If that had been the case, he would not have been commissioned! As it was he had to remain a cadet for an extra six months and thereby lost considerable seniority in rank. It all happened because of his infamous attack on a fellow (unpopular!) comrade whose backside was nearly set on fire by Monty! The victim was seriously hurt and had to go to hospital. If it had not been for our mother, who went immediately to Sandhurst and intervened with the Commandant, Colonel W.B. Capper, Monty would not have been allowed to join the British Army.

Monty's mother aged 43, when she went to Sandhurst to save Monty's threatened career.

Monty dressed for riding in plain clothes while staying at Hexham Abbey with his uncle and aunt, Canon and Mrs Savage.

British Officers of the 1st Battalion at Peshawar, 1909. 2nd Lieutenant Montgomery is clearly seen sitting in the front row.

That same year one of Monty's younger brothers, Desmond, then aged thirteen and a pupil at St Paul's School, died whilst under an operation to remove a mastoid infection from the brain; he was our parents' seventh child.

Opposite: Monty (standing right) shooting at New Park about 1908. Our eldest brother Harold is seated below him. Bowler hats for grouse shooting would appear strange today!

Monty finally left Sandhurst in 1908 and was commissioned in the Royal Warwickshire Regiment of British Infantry, then stationed at Peshawar in the North West Frontier Province of India.

Desmond Montgomery, born 1896, died 1909. He was a gifted and very good looking boy, with marked talents as a musician, particularly with the violin, at which he excelled.

Lieutenant Montgomery (smoking a pipe) with Tom and Tim Philby at Karachi by the gangway of *Northbrook*. They wear black armbands as King Edward had just died.

In 1910 Monty's regiment was posted to Bombay and moved there by sea from Karachi in the *R.I.M.S. Northbrook*, a ship of the Royal Indian Marine. This photograph is noteworthy, as it shows our family relationship with the traitor and Soviet spy Kim Philby! H. St J. Philby, the famous explorer and Arabist, was Kim's father and whose (maternal) great-grandfather was Henry Clare Cardew and brother of Mr Farrar, our grandmother. In the late 1960s this excited some public notice, including the fact that Monty had been best man at the marriage in India of Kim's father! Tom and Tim Philby were Kim's brothers, the former in the Royal Indian Marine and the latter in the York and Lancaster Regiment.

It was at Bombay that Monty had his first encounter with the German armed forces.

Regimental football team, Bombay 1911.

Monty was in charge of all regimental games when a German battleship, the *Gneisenau*, with the German Crown Prince on board, called at Bombay. A football match was arranged between the German naval crew and the Royal Warwickshire team, though Monty was strictly ordered not to field his 1st XI for the occasion; the German sailors were quite untrained for football but should not be seen to lose by too large a margin for political reasons. In the event, Monty fielded his very best 1st XI, and the British team won by the astonishing score of 40 goals to nil! Shortly afterwards Monty returned to the UK for six months leave.

n furlough in the UK in
911. He now has the thick
oustache often worn by
itish Army officers at that
ne.

In 1913 Monty's regiment
turned to England for
rrison duty at Shorncliffe
Kent, just 12 months
fore the First World War
gan in August 1914. He
ly went with his battalion
France as part of the
itish Expeditionary Force,
here, as a Lieutenant
mmanding an infantry
atoon, he had another
counter with the Germans,
the battle of Le Cateau. His
mpany had been ordered to
tack a forward German
sition and, later on, Monty
rote about it.

'Waving my sword I ran
rward in front of my
atoon, but unfortunately I
d only gone six paces
hen I tripped over my
abbard, the sword fell from
y hand (I hadn't wound the
vord strap round my wrist
the approved fashion!) and
ell flat on my face. By the
ne I had picked myself up
d rushed after my men I
und that most of them had
en killed.'

Thereafter, Monty took
rt in the famous retreat
om Mons and the Battle of
e Marne. However, on 13
ctober during fierce fighting
ound Meteren, he was
vice dangerously wounded
d very fortunate to be left
ive; a German bullet had
netrated and permanently
amaged his right lung,
aving him with only one-
d-a-half lungs for the rest
his life. But he survived
ry well, fully recovering his
alth and normal activity
d, in addition, had so
stinguished himself that he
as promoted in the field and
varded a decoration. The
mpaign in France and
lgium had not yet
veloped into the tragedies
trench warfare.

In the garden at Chiswick, March 1915, as Captain B.L. Montgomery DSO, and showing no sign of his recent wounds. Rank badges were still worn on the cuff.

ay 1915. Brigade-Major
1st Infantry Brigade, in the
K, commanded by
rigadier-General MacKenzie.
s uniform includes those
veted red collar tabs which,
those far off days, were
orn by all staff officers,
cluding ADCs, whatever
eir rank.
   In January 1916 Monty
turned to France as
rigade-Major 104th
fantry Brigade,
mmanded by Brigadier-
eneral Sandilands. In
ovember that year Monty
rote the following letter to
s eldest sister Una, who was
en living in Cairo where
r husband, Andrew
olden, was in the Egyptian
vil Service. I have quoted
is letter in full, with its two
otographs, as it shows his
ve and affection for his own
mily at the height of World
ar I.

Headquarters
104th Infantry Brigade
B. E. F.
17.11.16
My darling Una
   Very many thanks for
our letter and the
hotograph of you and
nity; it is very good I think
nd I shall like to have it
vith me. I hope to see you
ext year if you and Unity
ome home. I saw Donald
ut here the other day; his
rigade is only about 10
niles from me and I
notored over and had
unch with him. He was
ooking very well I thought.
   I enclose a photograph
aken by the local expert; it
s not bad I think. The one
f me alone shows the kit I
vear on a fine day and was
aken just before starting to
o round the trenches. The
ther one shews the
General and myself on our
eturn from the trenches on
very wet day. The short
oat and trousers (both of
ording Macintosh) keep
ne absolutely dry, and
fter long experience I am
onvinced they are the best
hings to wear in wet
veather.
   Love to you and Andrew.
      Yr loving brother
         Bernard

Photograph of Bernard, as mentioned in his letter to Una.

Photograph of Bernard with his General, as mentioned in his letter to Una.

Lieut.-Colonel B. L.
MONTGOMERY,
G.S.O.1, 47th Division

Mr. Winston
CHURCHILL,
Secretary for War

General Sir William
BIRDWOOD,
G.O.C. Anzac Corps

Opposite: This shows Monty (far right) with his elder brother Donald (far left) on the day that, according to his letter to Una, he lunched with his brother at the latter's headquarters. Donald was senior partner in a firm of well known solicitors in Vancouver, and had joined the Canadian Army at the outbreak of World War I. He won the MC in action and later returned to Vancouver, where he died in 1970.

Then in January 1917 Monty was promoted Major, at the early age of twenty-nine, and held staff appointments at both division and army corps level. Finally, in July 1918, Monty was promoted Lieutenant-Colonel and appointed GSO 1 of the 47th Infantry Division. It was four months before the First World War ended and his promotion had been very rapid. He began the War as a subaltern and, at its end, was the senior staff officer in a division.

October 1918. Ceremonial parade to celebrate re-entry into Lille in 47th Divisional area.

Churchill came from London to attend this occasion; it was the prelude to the victory of 11 November 1918 that saw the utter defeat of Germany.

This is the earliest known picture of the two men together – Winston Churchill and Monty, some 24 years before the Battle of Alamein. There is no evidence as to whether the two men actually met at Lille. For his service in France Monty was awarded the Croix de Guerre by the French Government.

For Monty the vital, personal lesson of the War was his utter determination that the terrible carnage, bloodshed and extreme suffering experienced during the trench warfare in Europe must never be allowed to happen again. This governed his thinking on warfare throughout all his professional life, and thereafter.

Meanwhile Monty's younger sister, Winsome, had been at Washington in the middle of the War when, as a young and attractive girl, she accompanied Bishop Montgomery on a two month visit to Canada and the USA.

Below left: Bishop Montgomery around 1916, when he made the tour to North America. Quite how he obtained permission to cross the Atlantic, with his daughter and at the height of the German submarine campaign, is not known.

Below: Old Lady Montgomery at Torquay where she died in 1919, aged 95.

Monty wrote about her, 'To the end she remained a very formidable woman, not to be trifled with at any time anywhere'! She was born into the East India Company scene and saw the 'Empire at war' for nearly a century.

Monty's mother, Mrs Henry Montgomery, in 1919 aged 55.

This is one of the few pictures in which she appears anxious or worried about something. No doubt because at that time three of her brothers, who were of course our uncles (and children of the great Dean Farrar), had shattered all the generally accepted rules and conventions by conduct which, in those days, was held to be outrageous – legally, morally *and* socially. Furthermore, all three were parsons and one of them, Percival Farrar, was chaplain to the Sovereign. But in his case, no one knew that Percival was a homosexual until he was caught in *flagrante delicto* with one of his own choir-boys! He had to leave the country immediately, whereupon he went to France and joined the Foreign Legion – certainly a tribute to his physical courage! He then served with merit and distinction during his five years in the Legion. Another brother, a rector in a country parish, was also found to be homosexual. The third (also a country parson) was prosecuted by his secretary in the courts for attempted assault, because he suggested that her salary should be paid, in part, by co-habiting with himself! Finally, one of mother's sisters, Evelyn Farrar, deeply shocked the entire family when she was converted to the Church of Rome. One of her sons also became a Roman Catholic and Benedictine monk.

The Rev. Percival Farrar, one-time Chaplain to the Sovereign and later of the French Foreign Legion. He is seen wearing the Foreign Legion greatcoat with its head dress.

It was Monty who was fond of referring to the three clergy as 'our wicked uncles'. However, in spite of the scandals, one should perhaps remember that all Dean Farrar's offspring were highly educated and extremely well read; they had learned to appreciate the arts, music, painting, sculpture, and the beauties of nature. The sons grew up in the age of, and often in company with, Oscar Wilde and Freud, and with painters like Moreau, Rossetti and Burne-Jones, whose works not infrequently carried their own homosexual implications.

Lieutenant Colonel B.L. Montgomery, DSO, Commanding Officer of the 17th Battalion Royal Fusiliers. 1919.

Soon after the Armistice, Monty was given his first experience of real independent command as a battalion commander at Duren in the Ruhr in occupied Germany. He enjoyed this very much for, as he told me later, 'I had already seen so many examples of how not to command a battalion'!

1920–1939

After the First World War, Monty attended the 1920 course at the Staff College Camberley. There he became unpopular with some of the directing staff by advocating abolition of the horsed cavalry, and their replacement by armoured regiments; in his view this was the only way to restore mobility to the battle field. From Camberley he was appointed Brigade Major of the Cork Brigade, in southern Ireland. This formation had nine infantry battalions and in reality was a division that was fully extended in operations against the IRA (Irish Republican Army) who were active against the British Government.

Major B.L. Montgomery DSO and Croix de Guerre, Brigade Major, Cork 1921–1923. He now has five medal ribbons in one line.

From Cork, Monty wrote to Bishop Montgomery at New Park on 1 March 1922, and I have quoted this letter in full as it shows the remarkable similarity between conditions in Ireland at that time and the British Army's operations in Northern Ireland since 1968; it also emphasises the human side of Monty's character and his deep affection for his father.

The bitter fighting in Ireland brought Monty one advantage. It was there, for the first time, he had met the officer who was to become his Chief of Staff for the greater part of the Second World War – Major General Sir Francis de Guingand, KBE, CB, DSO.

17th Inf. Brigade
Cork
1.3.22

My dear Father,

It is very difficult to find out how long they intend to keep us here in the south of Ireland. The situation is really impossible; we have had two officers murdered in the last fortnight; ambulances and lorries are held up almost daily by armed men and the vehicles stolen; the result is we now send armed escorts with every vehicle or body of men that leaves barracks, just as we did when the war was at its height. It is really more dangerous now than it was then, as we are now powerless; then we had martial law behind us and could do what we liked. The Provisional Government have no authority of any sort or description here; the south is entirely ruled by the Irish Republican Army who publicly state by proclamation in the local papers that they owe no allegiance to the Provisional Government, and that they adhere to the Republic. We have to be very careful as a false step would be a match that would set the whole country ablaze again. Our policy is that we do not care what any one does, or what happens, so long as the troops are left alone and are not interfered with; any civilian, or Republican soldier or policeman, who interferes with any officer or soldier *is shot at once*. The result is we are now left alone. Three armed civilians held up one of our closed cars the other day; they thought it was empty but for the chauffeur, and that they would be able to steal it. Unluckily for them there were three British officers inside it; they opened fire at once through the windows with revolvers; two of the civilians were killed, but the third escaped. It was a good lesson for them and they will think twice in future before they try similar hold-ups.

The IRA get no pay; there is no money to pay them with. They are now living in all the barracks in out-stations vacated by us. When they want money they go round the town and forcibly collect 5/- a head from every resident; this happens once a week.

It really is most degrading for us soldiers having to stay on here; and I shall be heartily glad to see the last of the people and of the place. Our presence here undoubtedly acts as a deterrent on the more extreme of the IRA, and I am sorry for the loyalists and others when we are gone. They get persecuted now but it is nothing to what will happen later. I fancy the elections will go against Griffiths & Co, and then there will be a nice mess.

Bolshevism is really the trouble here. No man wants to work when he can live for nothing in the IRA, and go round with a revolver when he wants money.

Have you heard the nonsense being rumoured about the burning of Cork? It is complete nonsense. Cork was burnt by K. Coy of the Auxiliaries*, and by no one else. A bomb was thrown into a party of them near Cork Barracks one night, wounding 14 of them. They broke out of barracks that night, and by the aid of petrol, etc., set fire to the City Hall and half the shops in Patrick Street.

I hope to get away about 7th April for a month's leave. The Army Golf Championships are on 24th April at Deal, and I want to get in some good practice before then. I shall go and stay at Camberley and practice there. Will you be in Town about 8th April?

Your affectionate son
Bernard.

* The Auxiliaries were a para-military police force, raised by the British Government after the 1914–18 war, and known in Ireland as the 'Black and Tans'. They were infamous for their tough and ruthless policy and much hated by the civilian population generally.

Freddie de Guingand as a young man.

My research showed the paucity of pictures in which both Monty and Freddie de Guingand appear: but the reason for this is clear. In war it was Monty's invariable rule to 'make his plan' and then leave it to the Chief of Staff to implement his orders. Thus, Monty and Freddie were not often seen together, and public knowledge and recognition of de Guingand's great and invaluable services to his country have suffered accordingly: too few people know about him.

Monty left Cork early in 1923 on appointment to comparative peace and quiet as Brigade Major, Plymouth; but not for long, as he was soon transferred to York as GSO 2 49th (West Riding) T.A. Division. There he lived at the depot of de Guingand's West Yorkshire Regiment, where Freddie was then also serving, so the two men were together for the next two years.

In the early 1920s, Monty generally went back to New Park during his annual leave.

Family group at New Park, summer 1924. Sitting, front row: my sister Winsome and Donald. Standing: Colin, Harold and Monty.

In 1925 Monty returned to his regiment at Shorncliffe as senior Major, and whilst there he fell deeply in love with a young and charming girl called Betty Anderson. She was a blonde and extremely attractive, but was still only seventeen, while he was thirty-eight.

Betty Anderson, *c.* 1925 . . .

Monty asked her to marry him, but the age gap ruled out any real prospect of her acceptance – fortunately, as it turned out for both parties. Two years later he did get married.

Below right: * David Montgomery in 1974; the year when he was President of the British Industrial Exhibition at São Paulo, Brazil.

Now the Second Viscount Montgomery of Alamein CBE.

Below: Mrs Bernard Montgomery (Betty Carver) in about 1930. She was about Monty's age, dark and vivacious, unquestionably a very charming woman and greatly liked by all.

They first met during a skiing holiday in Switzerland, she a widow with two sons by her first marriage to Major Carver, RE. She was very artistic and differed in every way from Monty, except in her very keen sense of humour. They were married at Chiswick Church on 27 July 1927. The couple began their married life at the Staff College Camberley, where Monty had been appointed an instructor the previous year.

Many (future) distinguished officers (men like Field Marshal Alanbrooke and General Sir Dick O'Connor) were fellow instructors at Camberley and Alexander was a student under Monty. The latter's son, David Bernard Montgomery, was born while Monty was still a teacher at the Staff College.

Opposite: Lieutenant Colonel B.L. Montgomery DSO, commanding officer 1st Bn Royal Warwickshire Regt. 1931. After his instructorship at the Staff College, Monty was given command of his regiment and served overseas in that capacity in Palestine, Egypt and India.

Jerusalem 1931, with two of his officers and the commandant of the Palestine Police Force.

Alexandria 1932. The winning team in the Egyptian Command tug-of-war competition. The regimental mascot was always a black buck from India (left foreground).

The Bishop and our mother, Mrs Montgomery, at New Park in their old age. The Bishop died in 1932, while Monty was in Egypt.

Opposite above: The Regimental drums and fife band in ceremonial tropical uniform. Monty is seated in the middle of the front row.

Opposite below: Monty at the Athletic Meeting 1932; a typical attitude.

Regimental sports. Alexandria 1932. The Colonel wins the Officers' Race!

Inspection by the Army Commander, Lieutenant General Sir J. Burnett-Stuart KCB, KBE CMG, DSO, in Alexandria 1933.

On leave in the UK at Bisley in Summer 1933. This photograph shows the commanding officers of both battalions of the regiment together.

Opposite above: Armistice Sunday (1918) Church Parade Alexandria 1933, marching back to barracks with Monty leading his regiment.

While he was in Egypt Monty pioneered the abolition in the Army of compulsory church parade services, which he thought should be made voluntary. They were.

Early in 1934 Monty took his regiment to India to join the brigade in garrison at Poona.

Opposite below: The officers of the Royal Warwickshire Regiment at Poona.

Later that year Monty was promoted to full Colonel rank and appointed Chief Instructor at the Staff College Quetta in Baluchistan in north-west India. The three years, 1934–37, that Monty and Betty spent at Quetta were among the happiest times of their marriage. They led a full and varied social life, whilst for Monty it was possibly the most significant period of his professional career between the wars.

		Lt	2/Lt	Lt	Lt	2/Lt	Lt		Lt	2/Lt		
Back Row:		Etches	Pocock	Besant	Burge	Holdich	Ferguson		Nicholson	Hyde		
	Lt	Lt	Lt	Lt	Capt	Capt	Lt	Lt	Lt	Lt	Lt/QM
Centre:	Jerram	Howes	Harborne	Rippon	Edwards	King	Willans	Poole	Bowly	Boyer	Mitchell
	Capt	Capt	Major	Capt	Lt Col		Major	Major	Capt	Capt	
Front Row:	Maunsell	Bailey	Anyvett	Catherall	Montgomery		Collins	Swinhoe	Edlin	Cubberley	

The bungalow at Quetta – known to this day as 'The Monty House'.

They lived in this pleasant though very old-fashioned, bungalow with a large garden. In the India of the 1930s, there were comparatively few modern amenities: no piped water supply, and roofs were of corrugated iron. 'The Monty House' is preserved for posterity as part of the Staff College Museum.

The Staff College Quetta as it was in 1934–37.

Staff College Quetta as it is today after modernisation by the Pakistan Army.

In May 1937 Monty returned to England and was promoted to Brigadier in command of the 9th Infantry Brigade at Portsmouth. Then fate struck him her cruellest blow – in the midst of high success. Suddenly Betty died of septicaemia in October 1937. Very few photographs of her survive, as all their possessions were still in store at Portsmouth where they were totally destroyed by a German bomber air raid in 1943.

In October 1938 Monty was promoted Major-General to command the 8th Infantry Division in Palestine, where the Arab rebellion was at its height. Monty sent me two photographs of himself in Palestine in the Spring of 1939.

Myself, the French C-in-C in Syria, and Brigadier Evetts. We are standing on Napoleon's Mound from which he reconnoitred for his attacks on ACRE. The town of ACRE is in the background. Gen. Cailloux is the French C-in-C. Lunch by the roadside near the Jordan valley.

When Monty arrived at Haifa to take command of the 8th Division, he was still quite unknown to any of his subordinate commanders. The following account of how Monty handled an ugly incident of the Arab rebellion shows his own manner of dealing with his subordinates, and his developed style of leadership, tactful yet decisive.

Lieutenant William Brown*, a junior artillery officer, had become involved in the *Suk* (Arab market) when shooting had started and 14 Arabs were lying dead in the street. The following morning Brown was told to report personally to his newly arrived divisional commander at Haifa. No one else was present when the following conversation took place.

MONTGOMERY: Your name is Brown, isn't it, Lieutenant Brown?
BROWN: Yes sir.
MONTGOMERY: What's all this I hear? That you are responsible for all that shooting yesterday, and that you've killed fourteen Arabs.
BROWN: No sir, that's quite wrong. The Arabs started the trouble.

Brown then gave the General an account of what had occurred, and finished by saying:

BROWN (contd): Look here, sir, I've been here now for eighteen months and I know personally what the situation is. You have only just arrived and you may not be aware that all British other ranks are fed up with being bombed and shot at, and yet not be able to take any retaliation. Not to fire back in the circumstances I have described would have been madness, sir. Besides look at the salutary effect it had . . .
MONTGOMERY (breaking in): Wait a minute, Brown. Your name is Brown, isn't it? What I want to know is: who is interviewing who? you or me? Now, listen to me. It is possible you didn't kill enough Arabs, though the result appears to have been good. On the other hand you may have been most unwise and acted very foolishly. I shall have to decide. That's all.

Brown saluted and went out. He heard no more of the affair, and there was no report of it in the press, or elsewhere.

It is now 1939 and the war years are about to begin again; but they started very badly for Monty, who suddenly developed a patch on his lung – a relic of his 1914 wound – and he had to be evacuated by sea to England as a hospital case.

---

* The Late Major-General W.D.E. Brown CB, CBE, DSO.

PHASE 1: 1939–1943

*Yet man is born unto trouble
as the sparks fly upward.*

The Book of Job v, 7

Monty wrote this quotation at the head
of the text of his *Memoirs*, published
after completing 50 years of
commissioned service. I have requoted it
here as it looks so apposite in the picture
of his life that followed after the
outbreak of war in 1939.

He recovered completely from the
illness which had sent him home from
Palestine. On mobilisation of the British
Army in August 1939, he was given
command of the 3rd Division that went
to France with the British
Expeditionary Force in September.
Because of possible censorship, I found
comparatively few pictures of Monty in
the so-called 'phoney war' in France or
thereafter, during the dramatic events of
the Dunkirk retreat and the threatened
invasion of England, until the summer
of 1942. I therefore turned to Monty's
Memoirs for any such 'blank' period. In
this context, I came to conclude
increasingly that to 'understand' fully a
picture, or portrait, you must look and
look again, particularly where the
spoken word is also quoted; after a
while, the reality and an increased
understanding begin to grow.

Date 19 November 1939 in France. 'Lord Gort (C-in-C the BEF) centre foreground, with Mr Hore-Belisha (Secretary of State for War) visited my 3rd Division area. General Brooke (my Corps Commander) can be seen behind and to the left of Hore-Belisha. I am on the far right wearing battle dress – the first General Officer ever to wear that dress.'

Outwardly Monty appears confident, unlike those around him. Yet beneath it he was indeed worried, for he wrote, 'It must be said to our shame that we sent our army into that most modern war (1939) with weapons and equipment which were inadequate, and we had only ourselves to blame for the disasters which overtook us when fighting began in 1940.'

France, December 1939. Lieutenant General Brooke, Corps Commander, with his officer commanding 3rd Division Major General B.L. Montgomery.

No book about Monty during the second world war would be complete without emphasis on 'Brookie' – the late Field Marshal The Viscount Alanbrooke KG, GCB, OM, GCVO, DSO – particularly as the latter, more than once, was personally responsible for saving Monty from being 'sacked'. The first such occasion was in France in 1939.

Monty was well aware of the increasingly serious effect of venereal disease in his division, as in others, because it caused so much absence from duty – *in war time*. He therefore issued an administrative order, with its sole purpose the need to reduce this casualty rate. The order, too long to quote in full, included his personal instructions to commanding officers in the following terms.

'. . . my view is that if a man wants to have a woman, let him do so by all means; but he must use his common sense and take the necessary precautions against infection – otherwise he becomes a casualty by his own neglect, *and this is helping the enemy*.

There are in Lille a number of brothels, which are properly inspected and where the risk of infection is practically nil. These are known to the Military Police, and any soldier who in need of horizontal refreshment would be well advised to ask a policeman for a suitable address.'

(signed)

Few, if any, complete copies of this order (Div. 179/A of 15 November 1939) exist. But it caused an immense uproar and a call, by the War Office, for Monty's replacement. Only Brookie's tact and support for Monty saved the latter from dismissal; he refused to withdraw the order, being quite sure that on this occasion, to appeal to the personal and private character of men was correct.

It is now a fact of history that early in August 1942, following the disastrous retreats of the 8th Army in Egypt (in Alexandria people could hear the sound of German artillery fire), Churchill had decided on drastic changes in Mid-East army commands; *inter alia* Alexander* was to become C-in-C Middle East whilst Monty was to be GOC 8th Army.

* The late Field Marshal Earl Alexander of Tunis, KG, GCB, OM, GCMG, CSI, DSO, MC PC, LLD.

Lieutenant General B.L. Montgomery arriving in Cairo, 12 August 1942, to take command of the 8th Army.

Of the many shots of Monty, I would suggest that this photograph shows certain outstanding characteristics: complete self-confidence in his own ability; complete determination to implement his own plans; and leadership – the inspiration which made his men follow him. That 'Montgomery nose' is plain to see!

In the dozen or so photographs which follow, these characteristics appear again and again, coinciding with the final defeat of the German and Italian armies in North Africa.

Below right: The newly arrived GOC 8th Army talking to officers.

Later he posed for this particular occasion to show the Australian head dress given to him by the 9th Australian Division.

Very early in the war he appreciated that, as in his case, leadership could include attitudes and behaviourism, which attract subordinates to you and earns their devotion and loyalty – allied, of course, with success.

Pursuing this policy Monty collected a series of regimental cap badges with which to emblazon his Australian hat. Showmanship maybe – but it certainly worked.

He had also adopted his famous black beret of the Royal Tank Regiment, to which he added the cap badge of a General. In all of British military history no other soldier has ever worn more than one badge on the front of his head dress.

Visiting the Greek Brigade of 8th Army, whilst also accepting their badge.

1 August 1942, talking to
General Horrocks, GOC 13
Corps, before the defensive
Battle of Alam Halfa, which
preceded Alamein.

30 August 1942. Further
planning for Alam Halfa.
Brigadier Roberts
commanding 22 Armoured
Brigade (far right holding
map), with General Horrocks
next to Monty.
   At that stage the only
available tanks in 8th Army
which could destroy the
German *panzer* (armoured)
troops, were the Grant tanks
of Roberts' brigade; hence the
importance of this
photograph.

Opposite above: First victory.
The Alam Halfa battle has
been won, 6 September
1942. Monty wrote:
'Rommel's doom was
sounded at Alam Halfa: it
was the turning point of the
desert war.'

Opposite below: The great
battle of El Alamein (23
October to 4 November) has
just begun. Here Monty
wrote on this photograph:
'Battle of Alamein; having tea
with my tank crew. On the
right is Lieutenant John
Poston (11th Hussars), my
ADC.'

A first essential at Alamein
was to clear the enemy
minefields through which
tanks could advance. Here
sappers of the Royal
Engineers are sweeping for
mines.

The infantry advance
preceded by an immense
artillery barrage.

The battle is going well, after much anxiety including changes in battle plans. Monty views the operations from his Grant tank.

In this picture I believe we see, in particular, immense drive and self-confidence in his own ability. He wrote: 'I was told by all and sundry about how I should fight the battle, what I ought to do next, and so on.'

Complete victory. Von Thoma, Commander of the famous Afrika Korps, surrenders to Monty at his Advanced HQ on 4 November 1942.

Monty's expression in this historic photograph deserves close study. The German General, formally dressed in uniform compared with Monty's jersey, has surrendered and is saluting his conqueror; whilst Monty, standing bare-headed with one hand in his pocket, makes no response – though with a mixed expression on his face, compounded surely of humour with some astonishment and relief, at this marvellous development.

Monty invited Von Thoma to dinner with him that night of 4 November, and also to breakfast the following morning.

he pursuit after Alamein
ontinues. The enemy lines
re cracking, his troops are
eeing westwards, leaving
housands of prisoners and
ead. Monty poses for this
hotograph, unconcerned by
nemy shells falling close
ehind him.

8 November 1942. Sollum,
n the frontier of Egypt with
bya, is recaptured.
   Monty is having a picnic
nch with his ADC. Of what
he thinking? His brain
ver tired, maybe because
 always went early to bed
d slept without any
fficulty. In this picture I
nse he is, first, looking back
 the amazing speed of
ents since he arrived to
ke over 8th Army; the
thority with which he had
anned, trained and
mmanded his Army at the
ttle of Alamein was his
eatest achievement so far.
irely his mind is also
nging over plans for
ntinued pursuit with the
m of forcing the enemy to
timate surrender.
   But he has been strongly
iticised for slackness and
lay in making that very
rsuit. Yet his critics forget
at Alamein cost 13,000
sualties. Monty knew his
my was still untrained to
 standard he required; he
ould not risk defeat.

Relaxation in Cairo. After Alamein, Monty used sometimes to return to Cairo for weekends of complete rest. His brother-in-law (Andrew Holden, in plain clothes) lived there, though his wife (our sister Una) was in England.

Pursuit of the retreating German and Italian armies went on, right across Tripolitania, until finally Tripoli, the key to conquest of North Africa, was captured.

23 January 1943. Another surrender, this time by the Italians. General Montgomery accepting surrender of Tripoli from the Lieutenant-Governor of Libya and the Chief of Police of Tripoli.

In both the German and Italian *surrender* photographs Monty's demeanour is markedly informal, still with left hand in trouser pocket, though with the Italians he wears uniform and the rank badge of a full General. This promotion, as well as a KCB, had come on 11 November 1942. Now he won't even bother to look at the Italians.

Tripoli, Monty relaxes in
e sunshine with a picnic
nch on the sea front, in
mpany with Lieutenant-
neral Oliver Leese,
mmander 30 Corps.
After Tripoli the end of the
ar in Africa came in sight;
t not before very fierce and
fficult operations, with
tter hand-to-hand fighting.
entually, the New Zealand
vision broke into and
tflanked the German
estern flank of the Mareth
ne defences, on 28 March.

April 1943. Monty
ngratulates the New
alanders and Armoured
vision troops, who carried
t that great outflanking
ovement, at Mareth; it
came known as 'Monty's
ft Hook'.

eutenant General Sir
rnard Freyberg, and
onty, relax together at a
ncert in the desert provided
the New Zealand Division
tertainment unit.

Above left: 31 March 1943. General Eisenhower arrives at 8th Army Headquarters to meet Monty for the first time in Africa.

Eisenhower made this visit as C-in-C All Allied Forces in North Africa, and therefore as Monty's boss. But it was not the first time they had met. 'Ike' had seen Monty briefly in England on 27 May 1942, when the latter was GOC south-eastern Army; subsequent events showed how the two men never agreed professionally. Meanwhile, enemy resistance in Africa ended on 12 May 1943. It was total victory, with 248,000 prisoners in Allied hands.

Above: Late May 1943. Two famous war heroes (Monty and Wavell) meet briefly in London.

Monty went to London for a short holiday after the desert war had ended; about this he wrote: 'One thing there made me feel lonely. An HMG Thanksgiving Service for victory in the war in Africa was held at St Paul's Cathedral. But, although in London, I was not asked to attend.'!

Left: Monty at the end of the African campaign.

Opposite: Monty in the UK in 1943 or early 1944, probably the latter.

This charming picture of Monty may well point to the reason why he was not invited to that Thanksgiving Service at St Paul's. At that time, and increasingly so later on, the movements of the top military commanders were highly classified for security reasons, and understandably so. But Monty personally was *always* good news, so his picture was used for PR reasons, but without giving any clue to his whereabouts.

Alexander and Monty visit Eisenhower's HQ in North Africa
confer together for the next operation – the invasion of Sicily
In fact they are deciding which photographs of themselves
they would like to see published!

10 July 1943. Picture taken in North Africa when troops of
8th Army were leaving for the sea-borne invasion of Sicily.
Monty is preparing to address his men as they embark in the
landing craft.

Opposite above: Monty speaking to men of the 11th Canadian
Tank Regiment near Lentine, Sicily, 25 July 1943.
   The Sicily invasion was the first time in the War when
Canadian troops actually fought in battle – under their gallar
commander General Simonds – and Monty recorded his high
appreciation of their morale and performance. They played a
major part in the hard and bitter fighting on the island.

Opposite below: Tac HQ in Sicily. Putting on his sweater befor
meeting the Press.

Monty gazing at his cage of captive birds, almost all budgerigars, taken on the island; the famous 8th Army Shield (a gold cross on a white shield on blue ground) has been fixed to the base of the cage.

The 29 August 1943 lunch party at Monty's HQ at Taormina after the final conquest of Sicily. Two armies (the British 8th and American 5th) won the campaign and this shows some of the commanders involved. Seated, left to right are: General Patton, Eisenhower and Monty. Behind Patton is General Bradley, and on the extreme right is (the British) General Dempsey.

The fighting in Sicily had lasted from 8 July to 17 August, and cost the 8th Army some 12,000 casualties, though almost half of these were due to malaria, not enemy action.

Opposite: Exactly four years after the day when war was declared against Hitler's Germany, on 3 September 1943 Monty goes back to mainland Europe, across the Strait of Messina, to launch the Allied invasion of Italy. Two years – all but four months – of much hard and intense warfare, in very arduous conditions, elapsed before all Italy was conquered.

B. L. Montgomery
General
Eighth Army
Italy
1943

Opposite: Southern Italy, 1943. The awful devastation of war.

About this time Monty's fame and ever-growing popularity began to rub off on our mother, living alone at our home in Ireland. She loved this reflected glory, and revelled in the attention paid her by the American armed forces in the UK! This following photograph shows what happened.

Our mother's visit to a United States Army Air Force base.

The seeds sown by this incident grew into family troubles between Monty and mother. During his official life he developed an obsession which caused him to object strongly lest any person (relative *or* friend) should appear to have any credit or recognition simply by being connected in some way with himself.

Meanwhile, Monty did not control strategy for the operation in Italy and therefore wrote about it. 'If the planning and conduct of the campaign in Sicily were bad, the preparations for the invasion of Italy . . . were worse still.' British historians have already said he was right: the near-disaster that befell the American 5th Army at Salerno in September is probably well known. However, there will never be Allied agreement on the matter. In the event, Monty spent only four months on mainland Italy, during which time the CIGS, General Brooke, visited the 8th Army.

Driving with General Brooke, 15 December 1943. Monty appears delighted – though the CIGS does not.

By then Naples had been recaptured and 8th Army had reached the Sangro river line. The Italian armies had surrendered, but the Germans had some twenty divisions in Italy, and were formidable opponents.

Major Richard Carver, OBE, Monty's stepson, who had been captured by the Germans in the desert campaign, has escaped and rejoins Monty.

Dick Carver was heading a reconnaissance party, which over-ran a strong enemy rearguard during the pursuit after Alamein, and he and his whole party were captured. Monty himself had been a few hundred yards to the rear, with only a small escort, and thus narrowly escaped capture! Carver had been handed over to the Italians in Italy, from whom he made a most daring and successful escape in September to rejoin Monty behind the Sangro River.

Colonel John Carver and his wife *c.* 1938. He is the elder of Monty's two stepsons, both of whom saw so much of Monty before war began in 1939.

At my Tac HQ after my farewell address to 8th Army at Vasto, 30 December 1943.' (Left to right) de Guingand, Air Vice-Marshal Broadhurst (Desert Air Force), Monty, Freyberg, two Corps Commanders (Generals Allfrey and Dempsey).

'Very early in the morning of Christmas eve 1943, I was woken up to be given a signal from the War Office to say I was to return immediately to England to command 21 Army Group, the British Group of Armies preparing to open a second front' across the Channel. Though sad of course to leave 8th Army I was naturally delighted to have been selected for the great task . . .'

Monty added: 'The really great hurdle which faced me was how to say goodbye to the officers and men of 8th Army, so many of whom had been with me since Alamein.' Indeed, the 8th Army had become almost a private club, with contingents in it from nearly every part of the Commonwealth and Empire. At its HQ there was the *expertise* of specialists, in addition to de Guingand, most of whom went on to persist with Monty until the end of the war. Richards, who controlled the armour, White the signals, Malise Graham the administration, Williams the intelligence, Belchem and others the operations, Kirkman the artillery; also there were many young colonels, majors and captains who had become avid disciples of the Montgomery technique. Finally the *corps d'elite* of generals in command of formations and divisions: Dempsey, Simonds,

Freyberg, Horrocks, Allfrey, Leese, to name but a few.

That 'Monty technique', was really a mix of components. First, the care he always took for the welfare of his troops (expressed in the magnetism of the man), which guaranteed their loyalty and, perhaps above all, their trust. Trust in his leadership, which meant their belief that in battle their lives would be as safe as possible in his hands. Furthermore, he acted as no British General had ever done before.

In the desert campaign and in Italy, having made his plan and given instructions to de Guingand, he would leave his HQ and motor many miles to the rear. He wanted to see for himself how his men were faring in the back area; he well knew that units employed on vital, but little publicised, tasks are liable to think themselves forgotten. He therefore went to find and see them, travelling with only a liaison officer and ADC, and a small escort. He would stop frequently on these expeditions, and have a friendly word with men employed at supply points, or in small working parties.

He would identify himself (though they all recognised the two-badge beret) and then tell them to gather round, whilst he briefly described the battle situation and how he intended it should develop. Before leaving he handed out cigarettes and asked if any man would like to have a message sent, by the army commander, to his wife or girlfriend. The effect was immediate, striking and like magic: the dividends enormous.

Monty talking, and giving out cigarettes, to the men of 8th Army.

Monty took with him to London on 1 January 1944, to begin planning the second front, six key officers from 8th Army. They were de Guingand, Graham, Williams, Richards, Belchem and Hughes the Head Chaplain. Of course, he also took with him his three famous caravans, which were part of his personal HQ in Africa and Europe. One vehicle was for his bed and his bath, another was his office and map room, and the third provided room for overnight guests. Two were captured from Italian Generals Messe and Bergonzoli, and the third was sent out from England. All three vehicles are now on permanent display in London at the Imperial War Museum.

Monty sitting on the steps leading to his office caravan. On the wall opposite are badges of all the regiments that fought under his command.

PHASE 2:   1944–1945

The final two years of the War represented the crowning glory of his years in command. Much has been written about those momentous times and events. What remains, over and above the military successes in Europe, are the personal aspects of his life at the time – and that curious echo from the past that sounded in the choice of location for the days of planning which preceded D-Day.

St Paul's School, West Kensington, London. Monty's Headquarters for the invasion of France.

Some 40 years had passed since Monty had gone to school daily from Chiswick, to hear prayers read in Latin by the High Master. Now from this same large building he was to plan the sea and airborne assault on the coast of France, and the subsequent ground operations. In 21 Army Group he eventually commanded two American armies, one British and one Canadian army, two American airborne divisions, and one British airborne division.

A prodigious amount of staff work, at all levels, was required before the mammoth preparations (all master-minded from St Paul's School) could be regarded as complete. For those five months before the invasion, Monty lived at Latymer Court, a block of flats just opposite the school buildings and allocated as both living accommodation for himself and an Officers Mess for very senior people.

A signed photograph of the conference in St Paul's School, preparing for D-Day. (Left to right) General Omar Bradley, Admiral Ramsay, Air Chief Marshal Tedder, General Eisenhower, Field Marshal Montgomery, Air Marshal Leigh-Mallory, General W. Bedell Smith

Admiral Sir Bertram Ramsay, with Monty. Ramsay was in charge of all naval operations for the seaborne invasion of Sicily, mainland Italy, and the Overlord landings on D-Day.

Although this picture was taken during the Sicily invasion, nevertheless it portrays so well the always close co-operation between Monty and his naval commander. Tragically, Bertram Ramsay was killed in action on land in January 1945.

Soon after he began his planning at St Paul's, Monty appreciated that his own ideas on leadership demanded that he should be seen by every officer and soldier under his command. As he had done in 8th Army, so he did now, abandoning all detail to de Guingand (and the Americans) whilst he visited every camp and garrison in the UK. Furthermore, to great astonishment everywhere, he extended this military technique to the civilian population, men and women, in all the ordnance factories and munition establishments in the land. 'They are as much involved as I am,' he said. 'They make the weapons, and ammunition I must have.' Again the magic worked; literally in the UK Monty became 'the nation's idol'!

Monty leaving the War Office, 14 January 1944; the crowd waits to see him.

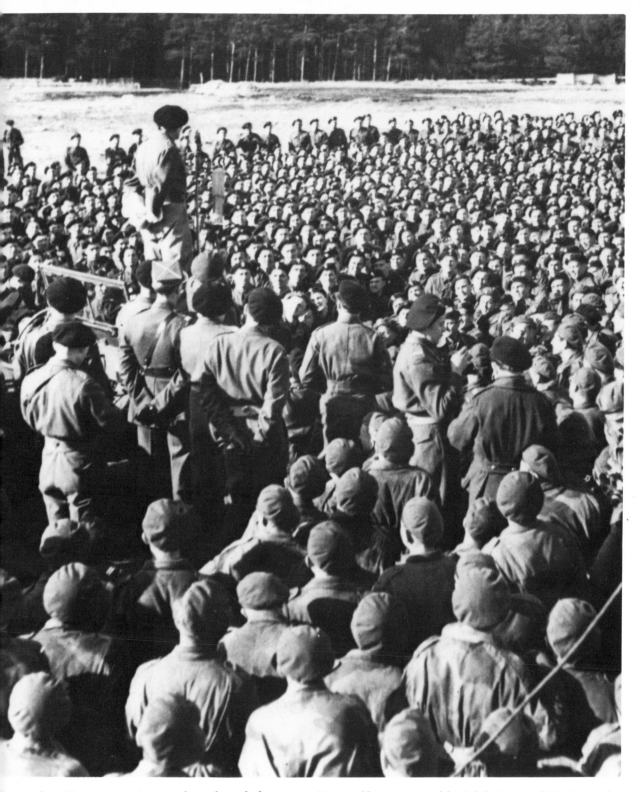

posite above: Monty signing autographs at the end of a
tball match, 4 March 1944.

Monty addressing men of the Polish Armoured Division in the
UK, April 1944.

posite below: Monty visiting a munitions factory, April 1944.
girl breaks from the crowd to shake his hand.

Bernard Montgomery.

Opposite: May 1944. He looks content with the approach of D-Day. Unusually, he has signed this photograph without adding his rank.

To ensure he could travel rapidly in the UK, with some comfort, Monty had a special railway train allotted to himself; this was kept at Addison Road Station for his sole use.

'The King comes to my Tac HQ to say good-bye before we go to Normandy, 22 May 1944.'

'The Prime Minister comes to dinner at my Tac HQ near Portsmouth, 19 May 1944.'

Conversation Piece supplied on a notable occasion, 9-11-44
an Attempt to persuade the unwilling soldier of the
importance of the beard as an attribute of greatness.

To F.M. B.L.M.

Opposite: Monty, before D-Day, while sitting for his portrait by Augustus John, with Bernard Shaw also present in the studio. Another painter, the late Sir James Gunn, was also there and left this charming pencil drawing of the unusual scene.

Monty never liked Augustus John's portrait of himself, or indeed the painter; he even refused to buy it, though a price had been named in the commission for the great artist. Monty gave his own characteristic opinion of Augustus John when he remarked, 'Who is this chap? He drinks, he's dirty, and I know there are women in the background'!

I shall limit my illustrations of the military detail of Monty's successful campaigns in Northern Europe to a few salient pictures; the events have already been prolifically photographed and published.

'The Prime Minister at my Tac HQ at Blay, West of Bayeux, on a wet day, 21 July 1944.'

The main interest in this photograph may lie in the utter informality of Monty's turn-out to meet the Prime Minister, dressed, in old corduroy trousers, creased jersey and unrolled umbrella, with that beret! But Churchill is in uniform – of a kind.

'Myself and General Bradley.'

Monty is wearing a Field Marshal's rank badge, so this photograph must have been taken after 1 September 1944, the day of his promotion. That was also the day when Omar Bradley assumed command of all American troops in France – the 12 Army Group. The two generals did not always agree – as perhaps this photograph may indicate!

After dinner at Monty's famous TacHQ, Belgium, September 1944; Brussels had been liberated. From left to right are: Monty, Kit Dawnay (Military Assistant), Eddie Brisk (standing, American Liaison Officer), Johnny Henderson (ADC), Tom Warren (Canadian Liaison Officer) and Noel Chavasse (Liaison Officer).

'Crossing the Seine at Vernon by a pontoon bridge, 1 September 1944.'

This date sealed the Allied victory and the expulsion of German armies from France. By 11 August the Americans had crossed the Loire, and Patton was racing for the Seine, which he had reached on 19 August. Paris fell on 25 August, Brussels was liberated on 3 September and Antwerp the following day. 1 September was also the day when Eisenhower had taken personal command of both 12 and 21 Army Groups. But before this there had been personal problems for Monty, particularly an attempt to replace him as responsible to Eisenhower for the operation of all British and American armies in France.

The late Marshal of the RAF, Lord Tedder, GCB, DCL, MICE, Deputy Supreme Commander to General Eisenhower.

It is not perhaps generally known how Lord Tedder strongly and consistently opposed Monty's plans, particularly their timing, which in the event was seen to be so successful. In a letter of 23 July 1944 Tedder had written:*

'I therefore urged again that Eisenhower himself should form a Tac HQ in France, and take control of the two Army Groups, thus putting an end to 21 Army Group's operational control over General Bradley's forces.'

Lord Tedder. Quoted from his *With Prejudice*, Cassell & Co, London.

Final victory is near. Lunching on *east* bank of the Rhine with Prime Minister and Brooke, 26 March 1945.

Winston Churchill insisted on visiting the battle area East of the Rhine. Later he wrote to Monty. 'I am so glad we had that day on the Rhine together, and saw a few shells playing about.'

At 6.30pm on 4 May 1945 (VE-Day) the German High Command signed an instrument of unconditional surrender, to Field Marshal Montgomery, of all German armed forces in Holland, north-west Germany, including all islands and ships in those areas, and in Denmark.

The following seven photographs illustrate the momentous event that took place on a hilltop on Luneburg Heath in northern Germany – near the little village of Wendisch Evern.

Left: Seven British soldiers who 'took command' of, and escorted, the German peace delegates from the battle front to 2nd British Army HQ: Major K.H. Freenan; Lieutenants M.E. Johnston and R.J. Frearson; Lance Corporals W. Peaple, H. Brennan, C. Flower, and Trooper R. Dawdry.

Opposite: Beneath the Union Jack the four German officers peace delegation are introduced to the Field Marshal. They are, from left to right: General-Admiral Hans von Friedeburg, and General der Infanterie Kingel with their staff officers Konteradmiral Wagner and (extreme right) Major Friedel
   The German officers are very well turned out. Monty, as usual, informal with hand in pocket and his expression – inscrutable?!

The German officers reporting to General Dempsey's 2nd Army HQ before moving on to Monty's Tac HQ.

Opposite: The moment of signing the surrender. Monty wrote, 'I had the surrender document all ready. The arrangements in the tent were very simple – a trestle table covered with an army blanket, an inkpot, an ordinary army pen that you could buy in a shop for twopence. I do not know what happened to that pen; I suppose someone pinched it. . . . The Germans were clearly nervous and one of them took out a cigarette; he wanted to calm his nerves. I looked at him, and he put the cigarette away.'

B. L. Montgomery
Field-Marshal.

B. L. Montgomery
Field - Marshal

HERE
AT 1830 HOURS ON 4TH MAY 1945,
A DELEGATION FROM THE GERMAN HIGH COMMAND
SURRENDERED UNCONDITIONALLY
TO
FIELD MARSHAL MONTGOMERY,
ALL LAND, SEA & AIR FORCES
IN
NORTH WEST GERMANY, DENMARK & HOLLAND,
&
SIGNED A DECLARATION TO THAT EFFECT.

Opposite: Monty on Luneburg Heath, and signed by himself that same auspicious day.

This is a picture, signed by Monty, of an oak plaque that was made, inscribed, and erected on the site of the surrender by the Royal Engineers, to commemorate the surrender.

Three days later this plaque was stolen, and of course replaced. On 24 September it was daubed with paint at night and removed, but later found 440 yards away and restored to its proper place.

The oak tablet, being cleaned by an ex-German wehrmacht soldier after it was found smeared by paint.

In November 1945, this wooden pillar was replaced by a permanent stone structure, weighing nine tons, quarried, fashioned and erected, again by RE, and faced with a new commemorative bronze plaque. However, on 4th May 1955, its tenth anniversary, the bronze plaque was stolen by unknown Germans who wrote on the stone, 'Due to this victory Communism could spread in the heart of Europe. After 10 years it is time to recognise the common danger. Let us forget the past.' Again, a new bronze plaque was made.

The final part in this strange story was not played until 1958, when the stone monument was removed by the RE, reconstructed and inscribed, and then installed in its now permanent home on the Square at Sandhurst.

However, in that first week of May 1945, war in Europe was almost over. Hitler was dead, Goebbels was dead. Himmler was in hiding, Goering a prisoner. The Russians were in Berlin and British troops had reached the Baltic. The German armies were streaming into the Anglo-American lines in front of the Russians; they had come first to Montgomery to offer their unconditional surrender.

1945–1951

War in Germany ended officially on 8 May 1945. But immense problems remained for Monty, who was appointed C-in-C of the British Forces of Occupation and British Member of the Allied Control Council in Germany. Meanwhile, in this British Zone, over one million civilian refugees were fleeing before the advancing Russians; one million German wounded were in hospital, and over one-and-a-half million unwounded German fighting men had surrendered and were prisoners of war.

For the next twelve months Monty had to work through top-ranking civilian advisers, who handled the vast political and administrative problems involved in governing occupied Germany. He had also to travel widely, including a victory celebration visit to Paris.

Opposite: Paris on the 25 May
1945. General de Gaulle
embraces Monty and invests
him with the Sash and Grand
Cross of the *Legion d'Honneur*

The following day, a huge
crowd of enthusiastic
Parisians gave a warm
welcome to Monty as he
drove down the Champs
Elysees in an open car.

Opposite: Monty's duties as Army Commander still continued. Early 1946, inspecting Military Training Centre at Bad Lippspringe. Left to right: Brigadier Harry Cumming-Bruce DSO, Seaforth Highlanders, OC Training Centre; Major-General C.M. Barber DSO, commanding 1st Scottish Division, Cameron Highlanders; Monty; Lt Col O.B. Laing, DSO, Instructor Training Centre, Cameron Highlanders.

From the outset in post-war Germany Monty had urged the creation of *one* Allied civil/military command under one (American) commander (Eisenhower), in the same way as the Russians had one single commander for all Russian-occupied Germany. But Monty failed and, in the event, there were three Allied occupation zones – American, British and French. This was the situation when Monty was ordered back to London to become Chief of the Imperial General Staff (CIGS) in the summer of 1946.

The CIGS. Back in the War Office, in the old building opposite the Horse Guards in Whitehall, 26 June 1946.

He has now reached the peak of his profession, having been nearly sacked several times, the first occasion while he was still a cadet at Sandhurst. He is a Field Marshal, CIGS, and head of the British Army. He had also, in 1946, been made a Knight of the Garter (KG) and created a Viscount of the UK. From 1946 onwards he continued to receive further honours and decorations.

Opposite above: Monty receives the Freedom of the City of London, Britain's highest civic honour, at a traditional ceremony in the Guildhall, 30 July 1946.

The Field Marshal was cheered by thousands of Londoners as he drove from Temple Bar through the streets of the City.

Opposite: Arriving at Hastings to receive the Honorary Freedom of the Borough.

Altogether Monty received the Honorary Freedom of over 50 cities, towns and boroughs in the UK and overseas; whilst more than that number of clubs, regimental associations and the like accorded him membership of their institutions. In addition he travelled widely, during his two years as CIGS, in order to visit as far as possible all units of the British Army, including the then very large Colonial Forces, wherever they were serving.

January 1947. Reception in Moscow by Marshal of the Soviet Union Josef Stalin.

Monty was determined to visit Stalin personally in the Soviet Union, and wrote to the latter asking if he would see him. Stalin agreed and the meeting took place: the first time ever that a British CIGS made an officially approved visit to Moscow, at the invitation of Marshal Stalin and the Russian Chiefs of Staff.

In London, Monty was living in a flat in Westminster Gardens, but he soon realised he now needed a permanent home for himself and his son David, who, after completing national service, was about to go to Trinity College Cambridge. He therefore acquired an old water mill, dating from the 17th century, that stood on the bank of the River Wey in the village of Isington in Hampshire.

Isington Water Mill as it was when Monty bought it in 1947.
    The building, which still contained all its old machinery, was uniquely situated on a triangle of land, with the main stream of the river on one side and the mill stream on the other.

Opposite: Isington Mill after it had been converted to become Monty's family home.
    There had never been a garden at the Mill House so Monty set about creating one of his own choice, chiefly lawns, rose trees and flowering shrubs. He had the river bed and mill stream completely cleaned out; the entire conversion was not finished until the early 1950s.

Opposite: Looking towards Isington Mill across the garden. The large barn on the right was especially built to house Monty's three war caravans.

The highly popular and much publicised annual Alamein Reunions, at the Royal Albert Hall in London, had begun, attended by thousands of ex-8th Army soldiers from the many nationalities involved. The picture opposite, taken at the reunion on 23 October 1947, must be unique! Inscribed by himself, Monty in the arms of that beautiful, famous and talented actress Greta Gynt.

A sequel, a few moments later. Readers will doubtless assess Monty's expression for themselves. Is there perhaps some embarrassment? Even some doubt about the next move?!

Following that momentous occasion at the Albert Hall (!) Monty departed for an extensive tour of Africa, and returned just in time to take the passing out parade of the Royal Armoured Corps OCTU at Bovington in Dorset. This was important, as David, his son, was receiving a National Service Commission and had passed out top from the training school at Bovington.

David Montgomery receives the Belt of Honour from his father, as the best cadet in the commission list from Bovington on 20 December, 1947.

In September 1948, Monty was appointed Chairman of the newly-formed defence committee of Allied Commanders-in-Chief of the Western Union, with Headquarters at Fontainebleu; this was the beginning of the organisation which later developed into Supreme Headquarters Allied Powers Europe (SHAPE) as part of NATO in Paris. General Eisenhower was the first Supreme Commander-in-Chief and Monty was his Deputy C-in-C with effect from 2 April 1951.

Mother in her old age. She died July 1949 at our family home in Co. Donegal, just as Monty was beginning his task at NATO.

She was a much loved and indomitable old lady who made her first flight in an aeroplane at the age of 78, though Monty seldom saw her after he became famous.

DEPUTY SUPREME COMMANDER
1951–1958

Monty much enjoyed his years at NATO largely because he travelled so extensively, visiting all the fifteen NATO countries and inspecting their armies and defence establishments. Furthermore, he also met and talked with those nations' prime ministers, high officials and soldiers, to persuade their governments to rebuild their military forces once again. His Supreme Commanders were, first, his old chief General Eisenhower, and then in succession Generals Matthew Ridgeway, Alfred Gruenther, and Lewis Norstad.

All four Generals of the Army (the highest American military rank) were very pleased that Monty should tour

Europe as he did. For his prestige as an international soldier was enormous, and his reputation as a high-ranking officer, able to advise on every aspect of a nation's defence needs, was equally high. It was this aspect of his NATO task that went a long way towards reconciling him to the fact that, professionally, he was no longer a general officer, Commander-in-Chief; he could not give orders to troops. His role was more that of inspection and advice to all NATO armies, with, above all, the need for hard and sound training and organisation, and the inculcation of leadership and morale at all levels.

[Op]posite: Arriving at SHAPE [he]adquarters in Paris on his [firs]t day as Deputy Supreme [Co]mmander.

[Ge]neral Eisenhower arrives [in] Paris and meets Monty at [th]e Raphael Hotel. On the far [lef]t is Colonel Costa de [Be]auregard (Monty's French [AD]C) and on the far right [Ad]miral Carney, USN C-in-C. [ ] Because of his travels [M]onty was not often in Paris [an]d he seldom slept there, [be]cause of the generous and [pa]triotic gesture of a wealthy [an]d aristocratic French [ci]tizen. This gentleman had [de]cided to offer his family [ho]me, the beautiful Louis [X]III Chateau de Courance, as [th]e living place of Field [M]arshal Montgomery. This [lo]vely residence was about [h]alf-an-hour's drive beyond [th]e city limits, and Monty [to]ok full advantage of the [w]onderful opportunity for a [q]uiet and peaceful life after [of]fice hours in Paris. He lived [th]ere very comfortably with [h]is two ADCs (one British [an]d one French) and a very [a]dequate house staff; the [b]eautiful gardens were [m]aintained to perfection.

[T]he Chateau de Courance, [w]ith its lovely curved [ba]lustrade leading to the [m]ain entrance.
[ ] Monty took virtually no [p]art in the social life of [S]HAPE and very seldom [at]tended any official [en]tertainment; he did [h]owever give a large cocktail [p]arty at the Chateau once a [y]ear.

Talking to his soldier servant in his bedroom at the Chateau. Monty always took the greatest care with his turn-out in uniform at SHAPE.

Opposite: Walking with the late General Sir Brian Horrocks along one of the tree-lined avenues. The staff follow behind.

Monty very much enjoyed entertaining his old friends, or his official guests, *privately* at the Chateau. He kept a very good table there and always insisted that the food and wines should be of high quality in keeping with the scale and style of his residence; his great sense of humour was much to the fore when visitors came, as they did very frequently.

Whenever time permitted Monty returned to England and invariably stayed at his home at Isington Mill.

Talking with the French postmistress when the mail arrived at the Chateau. Monty always protested that he spoke French; in practice he spoke only English!

At the Mill. A Portrait in oils painted by General Eisenhower and presented by the latter to Monty.

Monty was very proud of this portrait and hung it in a prominent position in his study; he is seen wearing service dress uniform with no medal ribbons except that of the United States DSM. On the mahogany chest immediately below are framed photographs of himself, Bishop Montgomery, and of his own crest and coat of arms; also some of the caskets presented by cities upon granting him their Freedom.

Monty inside one of his caravans. He always went there whenever he came back from Paris.

Saluting the Alamein Memorial in 1954 in the Western Desert after placing his wreath at its foot. Thus, twelve years after the desert campaigns, Monty unveiled a memorial to the near 12,000 Commonwealth servicemen who died in the Middle East and have no known graves.

Monty comes to England in 1954 to take the Sovereign's Parade at the Royal Military Academy, Sandhurst.

In London at the Coliseum 28 May, 1953. Monty accompanied Sam Goldwyn to attend the film premier of *Guys & Dolls*. The ladies left to right are: Mrs Douglas Fairbanks, Jnr, Lady Templer

SHAPE was then primarily an international headquarters, essentially American in character and practice, and which Monty, with his direct *British* approach, did not exactly care for. He tended to feel frustrated, say on returning from a lengthy official tour, to find an office routine and procedure which he did not appreciate. His reaction, in the form of minutes which he addressed to the Chief of Staff at SHAPE, certainly startled the Headquarters! Below is an example:

Chief of Staff,

Have you seen the attached – paper for Council.
   If we have a prize list at SHAPE I would give it 1st prize, and an Olympic Gold Medal, for the maximum number of platitudes, long-winded sentences, unusual words, which many will not understand, and verboseness . . .
   I hope the Almighty will attend the Council Meeting when this paper is discussed. His help will certainly be needed.
   Montgomery of Alamein
   Field Marshal

No doubt it was more to his liking when he returned to England for events of the kind portrayed here.

Laying the foundation stone for a new church hall at St Mark's Parish Kennington, where Monty was born – in that large bedroom overlooking the garden.

The High Master of St Paul's School (Mr A.N. Gilkes) and Monty, in 1956 unveiling a D-Day plaque inscribed in Latin. This plaque was placed over the chimney piece in the school Boardroom. He had never entered this room as a schoolboy, but had taken it over as his private office in 1944.

Monty addressing the ship's company of the Battle class destroyer *HMS Alamein* in 1957.

Altogether Monty spent ten years' service in Paris (1948–1958). Towards the end of that period he left the Chateau (when the owner returned there) and lived, very comfortably, in a private suite at the Hotel Trianon Palace in Versailles. He liked to call from time to time at the British Embassy, where it was said that the only woman he really liked to sit next to at dinner was Nancy Mitford, who had settled in France.

Monty with senior officers at SHAPE. (Front, left to right) General Norstad, USAAF, General Gruenther, Field Marshal Montgomery, Admiral Sala, French Navy. (Back) Air Marshal Constantine RAF, General Schuyerler, US Air Force, General Brisac, French Air Force, Air Marshal Campbell Royd, Canadian Air Force. Both Gruenther and Norstad became Supreme Commander.

By 1958 Monty had completed 50 years of commissioned service since he left Sandhurst in 1908; he was also 71 years of age and still holding an official and very active appointment. But the authorities decided it was now time he retired from SHAPE!

However, in his capacity as a British army officer he could not, *de facto*, retire. For no 5-star ranking officer of the British armed forces can retire on pension; he remains on the active list and draws his pay for life, though the time may come when he is no longer actively employed in his service. Monty had now reached that stage, and of course many appropriate ceremonies and parades were held in the SHAPE countries to mark the occasion. France, in particular, paid him a most significant honour by awarding him their Medaille Militaire, a

very high distinction reserved only for French soldiers in the ranks and *not* their officers; exceptionally it is awarded to general officers who have been in command of armies. Its award to a non-French national indicates a rare exception for extreme merit.

History will surely acclaim Monty, in particular, for one great service to NATO. From 1948 he wanted Western Germany in NATO as completely and rapidly as possible. He had no doubts whatever on this score. It was no good retaining war time hatreds; Germany inside NATO would be invaluable, Germany outside NATO would be a menace. Subsequent events have proved how right he was.

Opposite: 19 September 1958. Monty inspects the Guard of Honour on his arrival at Lancaster House for the luncheon given him by HMG to show their appreciation of his 50 years' service to the nation.

Monty on 20 September 1958 when he returned to his home
at Isington Mill – for his 'so-called' retirement – for he
continued in a very active role.

During the ten years that followed his retirement, Monty systematically developed his own, and for him a new, way of life. He based himself at The Mill, the home of his own creation, where he loved to entertain his many acquaintances in all walks of life.

Distinguished soldiers, sailors and airmen, ministers of Government and politicians, famous historians, writers and journalists, all came to see him and seek his advice. Furthermore, he was able to enjoy activities which military service had denied him, and to relax.

Snooker, which he had not played for years but certainly played well now.

Opposite: Dressed in his robes as a Knight of the Garter (KG). Whenever possible he attended the annual service of the Order in St George's Chapel at Windsor Castle.

But no longer having any official duties, Monty particularly enjoyed the opportunities of meeting his own personal friends, particularly people like the Hamiltons, who had figured so largely in his life since the end of the Second World War.

Sir Denis and Lady Hamilton at their London flat in Palace Street.

Monty first met Denis Hamilton in 21 Army Group when the latter was commanding officer of his regiment, the Durham Light Infantry, on the invasion beaches in June 1944. Later he commanded a battalion of the Duke of Wellington's Regiment in the action that ended in the final capture of Arnhem.

Lieutenant Colonel Denis Hamilton, Commanding 7th Battalion, Duke of Wellington's, a few minutes before the battalion crossed the Ijssel and liberated Arnhem in April, 1945.

Hamilton was a professional journalist and an officer in the Territorial Army before the Second World War, during which he served with high distinction, won the DSO in 1944 and returned to journalism in 1946. He and Monty had taken to each other from the start, and they soon met again when Monty was CIGS and Denis was rapidly climbing to the top of his profession, in which he became very famous and earned a deservedly high reputation.

elaxing with the Hamiltons on a fine summer day at their
ountry house in Sussex.

It was occasions such as this that Monty probably enjoyed
ore than anything else. The Hamiltons went frequently to
he Mill and Monty used to stay at their Westminster flat
hen he had to go to London and stay overnight. It was
amilton who realised that Monty, once he had left NATO,
ight find it difficult to accept the sudden change from high
ffice, with all the facilities he had enjoyed; clearly his old
iend would need some new outlet for his still undiminished
nergy and incentive.

So it was Hamilton who gave Monty the idea that he might
ell find it rewarding to consider his future in terms of foreign
avel, broadcasting, writing and the like. Hamilton also
ayed a major part in the project that resulted finally in the
odging of Field Marshal Montgomery's personal war diaries
f both World Wars) in the safe custody of the Imperial War
useum.

Against this background, Monty's life became a very active
ne, particularly in those suggested three fields. Every
alendar year between 1959 and 1967 he visited a foreign or
ommonwealth country, often for several months; and of
ourse he inevitably met the Head of State, or the British
mbassador, and had long discussions with them. This
ometimes embarrassed the British Government as he always
wrote his reports' to the Secretary of State, though he was not
sked to do so and had no official rôle to criticise or comment
pon anything he had seen or heard – he was on holiday! His
rst such journey was to the Soviet Union, which he had
isited when CIGS.

pril 1959, leaving Downing
treet (properly dressed, with
owler hat and rolled
mbrella) after seeing Prime
Minister Harold Macmillan
bout his forthcoming trip to
Moscow.

First meeting with Soviet
Prime Minister Nikita
Khruschev, in the Kremlin.
His travels included visits
to India, Canada, China,
Central America (Honduras,
El Salvador, Guatemala,
Nicaragua), South Africa and
Egypt. In the 1960s the mail
steamers were still making
their weekly 11-day journeys
to Cape Town and Monty
took full advantage of that;
for six years he always spent
the worst months of the
English winter in South
Africa, travelling each way in
great comfort in a Union-
Castle line ship.

When going by sea to Cape
Town, he always had a
double first-class cabin to
himself.

Opposite: In South Africa
1962, enjoying the sunshine.

In the mid-1960s his old friend, the late Lieutenant General Sir Brian Horrocks, KCB, KBE, DSO, MC, LLD, came to see him.

Monty had already published his famous *Memoirs* (in 1958) which were translated for sale in the languages of all NATO countries. Now, in between his travels, he wrote and published four more books, in which he recorded the details of all his major journeys. In so doing he not infrequently brought trouble on his head because of his forthright comments on, *inter alia*, United States policy and leadership during the 1939–45 war. He also spoke frequently in the House of Lords, where equally he was not slow to speak his mind about controversial matters and people! On one occasion his speech brought him, potentially, into a very dangerous situation about which he wrote to me.

Dear Brian,

Enclosed letter seems to be up your street. It may have some connection with my speech in the Foreign Affairs debate, when I said we cannot have ONE Germany, and we should give *de facto* recognition to East Germany; or it may have some connection with the 'weed-killer'' remark.

Yrs ever,
Bernard.

---

30 March 1962
Field Marshal Montgomery
London

Dirty Bastard,

We come over soon. We spit you in your face. We bomb you with shit. You shithead. You are a war criminal and a criminal gangster. Attention: Plastic bombs will make an end to your life. Your house will burn down soon.

You are the most miserable creature living in Britain, you must be killed soon. And you will be.

The German A O S
Executive

The envelope of this letter was franked on the reverse as sent by 'F. M. Douglas, Park Hotel, Dusseldorf'.

The 'weed-killer' remark had been included in an address to officers at the Royal Military College of Science, in which Monty, reviewing the European military-political scene, had said:

'Dr Adenauer, Chancellor of the West German Republic, needs a dose of weed-killer. He's an old man and over-sensitive. A small dose would do.'!

Adenauer was then 87, and had been Chancellor for the past thirteen years. Of course, this remark provoked considerable trouble for the British Government and the official authorities could see no humour in it! Later the Security departments and the Chief Constable of Hampshire reported that the German AOS were a dissident and subversive organisation, though the originator of the letter was never identified.

Meanwhile, Monty continued writing, and also began broadcasting (not confined to military topics), both on television and sound radio. In the event he became quite expert and the BBC made occasional use of his services, with Jack de Manio, and other celebrities, interviewing him. His voice was popular, and people liked to listen to him – and he too liked to listen to his own voice!

Looking at the broad picture of Monty's life, after he finished his official career, probably his most interesting experiences were the two visits he made to China in May 1960 and September 1961.

Arriving in China and the first meeting with the Chinese. From their expressions it would be rash to conclude which party was the more surprised!

Monty had written to the Head of State, Chairman Mao Tse Tung, asking if he could visit China, and to which the Chairman had agreed at once. Monty was flown over large areas of Chinese territory, but of course he was only allowed to see what his hosts wished him to see. On one occasion he was taken by Chairman Mao to the Yangtse Kiang to watch the ruler of China swimming in the great river. Photography by foreigners was not then allowed.

In South Africa, visiting a black township near Cape Town.

Whichever foreign country he went to Monty always interested himself in its national and international problems. He had been to see Dr Verwoerd in Cape Town.

'Holding the baby!' Monty
meeting his first grandchild,
Henry David Montgomery*,
born 1954.

In 1953 Monty's son David
had married Mary Raymond
Connell, younger daughter of
the late Sir Charles Connell,
and in the next picture we
see Monty with his son and
daughter-in-law Mary, who
is holding their son Henry.

* Now the Hon. Henry Montgomery,
  heir of his father the Second
  Viscount Montgomery of Alamein.

In due time Mary
Montgomery had her second
child, a daughter Arabella
Clare, who is seen in the
immediately following
photograph.

Grandfather again, with Henry Montgomery and his sister, Arabella, in the garden at The Mill, 1959. This charming and wonderful photograph was taken on a summer's day by Antony Armstrong-Jones (before he became the Earl of Snowdon), who visited Monty and took this and other photographs.

Monty's last tour abroad, lasting ten days, was made in 1967 when he revisited all the Western Desert region of the great battle of El Alamein; and 25 years after that world-famous event was an appropriate time. He had written *privately* to the Head of State, the President of Egypt (Gamel Abdul Nasser) requesting permission for the visit, but without telling HMG, or the British Embassy in Cairo! Such action was again not popular in Whitehall, the more so because of the elaborate military reception Monty was given on his arrival in Cairo – at a time when political relations with Egypt were particularly delicate! (The seven day Israeli-Egyptian war began just a month later.)

Monty had taken with him to Egypt two of his 8th Army comrades, General Sir Oliver Leese and Brigadier H. S. Mainwaring, as well as Sir Denis Hamilton, then editor of the *Sunday Times*; indeed it was Hamilton's influence that made the tour a practical proposition, for his newspaper paid for the whole cost of the journey by air to Egypt and return to London, for the entire party.

Denis Hamilton. A happy sequence followed for the Egyptian Government then offered to pay all the cost of accommodation, travel and maintenance incurred by the party in Egypt.

Opposite: Heathrow 1967, returning from one of his last journeys overseas. Though he always travelled in great comfort, these tours were exhausting, and he is beginning to show some signs of fatigue. He was then 79.

At Alamein during the Egyptian tour. Monty, Denis Hamilton, Oliver Leese and Hugh Mainwaring find the exact site in the desert of their Tac HQ camp, on the day when Winston Churchill arrived.

Dame Vera Margaret Lynn, DBE, talking to Monty at the Alamein Reunion (Savoy Hotel) in the mid-1960s.

Vera Lynn 'The Forces' Sweetheart provided just that touch of glamorous memories which men and women need in war, particularly when far from home. Her record *Auf Wiederseh'n* sold over 12 million copies.

Opposite: Monty, photographed at home at The Mill in mid-1967.

Behind him is a portrait of himself by Frank Salisbury; in the author's opinion it is the best portrait of Monty painted during the 1939–45 war.

Saturday, 17 November 1967 was Monty's 80th birthday and to mark this auspicious occasion his old friend 'Simbo' – General Sir Frank Simpson, GBE, KCB, DSO – who was then Governor of the Royal Hospital Chelsea, gave a dinner party at the Governor's House. A dozen or so of the Field Marshal's closest friends were present, and Monty motored that afternoon to Chelsea where he was to stay with the Governor and Lady Simpson. That night burglars came to The Mill. The fact of the birthday was no doubt well known and his intended absence assumed, if not already known, and plans for clandestine entry possibly made accordingly.

The thieves broke in through the double garage which adjoined the house, and from which an unlocked door led into the entrance hall. The three members of the domestic staff, who lived in a servants' wing separated from the rest of the house by a passageway and a stout wooden door, heard nothing. Evidently the burglars were experts, for they searched for and took all the gold, silver and precious stones in the house; nothing else. They made no disturbance or noise and left no mess. Their loot included silver boxes and caskets presented with the Freedoms of cities, gold cufflinks and pencils; the insignia of the Order of the Garter and of other Orders, both British and foreign, some studded with rubies and diamonds worth thousands of pounds.

1967, at the Highland Division's Reunion in Scotland. General Sir Douglas Wimberley, Monty, General Sir Gordon MacMillan of MacMillan.

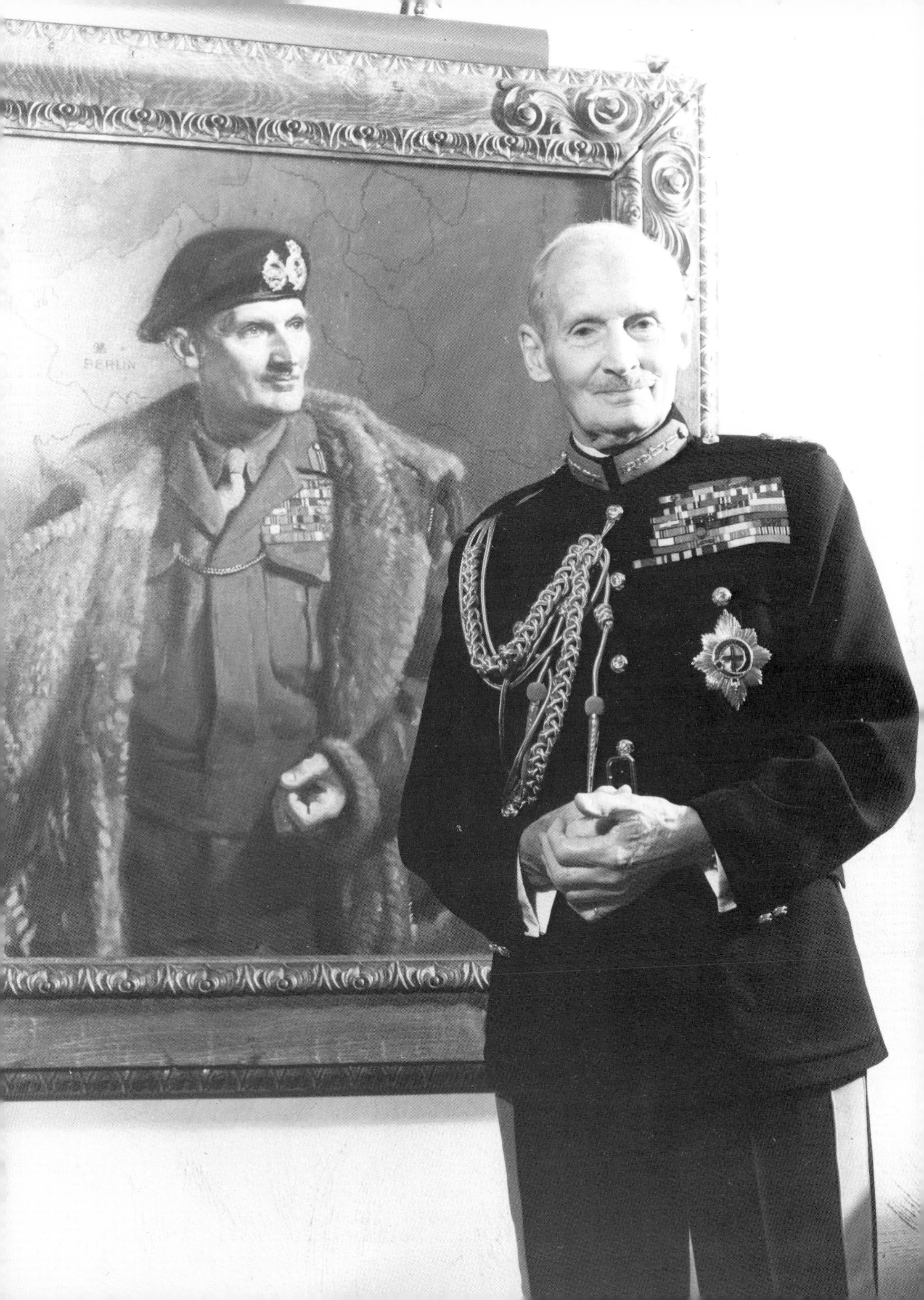
BERLIN

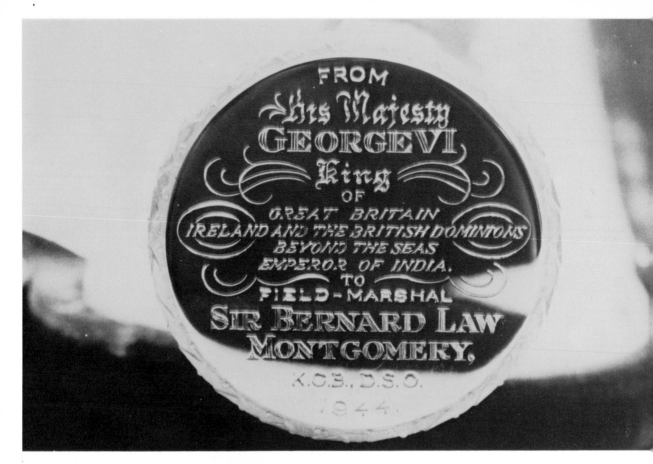

The most serious loss, a grievous one, was the Field-Marshal's baton, 23 inches long and covered with crimson velvet studded with 18 lions in gold thread. At either end is a flat boss of 18 carat gold, the upper of which is ornamented with figure of St George and the Dragon, also in gold. The base of the lower boss is circled with laurel leaves, chased with rose, shamrock and thistle; on the gold of this lower boss there is an inscription by HM King George VI, with the wording plainly seen in the photograph. The King had personally presented this baton to Monty at a private ceremony at Buckingham Palace in 1944. In spite of intense international police efforts nothing from this most dastardly crime has ever been recovered, and there is no evidence to indicate the identity of the thieves.

After the burglary Monty wrote the following letter to the author:

Isington Mill
12.12.67

My dear Brian,
    You and Bunty may care to have this coloured photograph, taken in my dining-room alongside the painting of our father – on the morning of my birthday and before the burglary. It is my Christmas present to you both.
                                            Yrs ever,
                                            Bernard

Copy of the picture, from the front jacket cover of *A Field-Marshal in the Family*.

David and Tessa Montgomery
c. 1971/72. In 1967 David
Montgomery's marriage was
dissolved, and he married,
secondly in 1970, Tessa,
daughter of the late General
Sir Frederick Browning and
his wife, the famous writer,
Daphne du Maurier. They
now live at The Mill.

This picture was taken on
American Independence Day
(4 July) in the early 1970s, to
signify the continuing RAF
and United States Air Force
co-operation.
   This was one of the last
public ceremonies attended
by Monty. The photograph
was taken at Chelmsford,
outside Essex County Hall,
during a joint Fly-Past by
RAF and USAF aircraft.

Monty in his garden in summer-time, during what he called 'the evening of life'. He was so happy there.

That Mill stream ran under the house and joined the River Wey on the other side – not visible in this picture.

Looking back, clearly Monty's health began its slow deterioration from 1969, when his doctor advised him not to make the visit he had arranged to New Zealand and Canada. Increasingly, he remained in the quiet setting of his home, with comparatively few visitors except for members of his family, and his close friends and companions from his wartime days. But he did spend a fortnight or so every January at the Carlton Hotel in Bournemouth, where some of his old friends were invited to join him; that great historian the late Sir Basil Liddell Hart and Lady Hart were generally there.

Gradually, he grew weaker until eventually he could not leave the house. Then finally he could not leave his bed, and for the last month or so he was scarcely conscious.

His last day on this earth was 24 March 1976. It was so quiet and peaceful, and only my wife and I were at his bedside when, at 1.30 am, he just gave a little sigh and 'crossed over Jordan'. He had often talked about death, and always phrased it that way.

As a Field Marshal, and a Knight of the Garter, Monty was given a solemn, military and ceremonial State Funeral at St George's Chapel in Windsor Castle. It was a truly magnificent occasion and all the 'great ones' of our nation, and of the British Commonwealth and foreign countries, were present or represented. The dress for the day was full ceremonial order, with decorations and medals worn by all ranks of the armed forces on parade. The procession formed up at Victoria Barracks Windsor and marched from there, in slow time, to the Castle. The two following pictures provide a sufficient display of the scale and size of this wonderful farewell. Monty was a great showman, as we have seen in this volume. He would have been so pleased to see this tribute to his leadership and courage.

Opposite above: The Funeral Procession in Windsor town.

Opposite below: Monty's last parade. At the Great West Door of the Chapel at Windsor Castle.

The final accolade of a moment's silence in funeral scene in
St George's Chapel, Windsor Castle.

THE SOLDIER'S GENERAL
(I wrote this in early 1983 BM)

In our house in Chelsea we have a portrait of my grandfather, Sir Robert Montgomery. It is an oil painting on wood, in a rectangular gilt frame of the kind so popular with family portraits in the Victorian era; it hangs on the wall at the foot of the staircase facing the front door. It is a half-length portrait in which he appears in evening dress, and just showing the crimson ribbon of the badge of the KCB, suspended round his neck. We do not know the identity of the artist, but he must have painted the picture well over a hundred years ago. He has shown my grandfather in a benign mood, but with a posture in which his eyes appear to dominate the scene; and if one lives with the picture it is easy to imagine that he is watching all that goes on in the house!

It was the 1 April 1976, and the garden was already a mass of yellow daffodils approaching their full bloom, though it was still very cold and there was no sun with low cloud cover. I had woken early for the day was going to be very important. In fact it was our wedding anniversary, but, with other members of the family, we were going to Windsor Castle for the State funeral service of my brother Field Marshal Montgomery. It would certainly be a novel experience for us, and I, with my nephew and his son, were to march, in slow time, with the Funeral Procession to St George's Chapel in the Castle. As I went down the stairs to get our early morning tea I felt grandfather was watching me and I seemed to hear him say: 'There's no need for any concern. I had to do all this, so many times, long before you were born.'

The magnificent splendour and precision of the State Funeral, with the brilliant colours of full dress uniform, the many thousands of people who came to Windsor, and the solemn service, are all unforgettable. But what followed is equally a treasured memory though so different in style. None of it appeared later in the press or on television or radio.

There were some five motor cars in the procession that conveyed the hearse, with the Bearer Party of the Coldstream Guards, the family mourners and the traffic police escort of motor cyclists, to the burial ground at Binsted Church. The drive was about thirty miles, through the quiet countryside of Berkshire, Surrey and Hampshire, with fields and woodlands already showing the first sheen of spring. The wind had dropped and the clouds had lifted though there was still no sunshine. We drove slowly, and in every village and hamlet through which we passed the people, men, women and little children, were lining the street as the funeral cortege went by. They stood quietly with heads bare, all the traffic had stopped and there was a great stillness, with no sound; it was the same in the open country, where cyclists dismounted and the passing motorist halted. At every village school the pupils, boys and girls, had left their classes and stood outside in ranks, in silence, with their teachers.

At Aldershot, the General in command had turned out the garrison to line the road along the route. It was not like the grand ceremony and parade at Windsor Castle, but simple and equally effective, very moving and quiet. All the troops wore their working dress – their dress for the day – the paratroops in their red berets, the Army Physical Training Corps, the RAMC, RASC, RAOC, REME, RAEC, the Provost Corps, all the services, with the WRAC, and also the NAAFI; they were all there. No commands were heard, but officers saluted and men with rifles presented arms; otherwise all ranks just stood at attention as the great soldier passed by on the way to his last resting place on earth. When we reached the burial place the sun came out.

It must have been evening when we returned home. We were all rather tired and were having the drink we badly needed. Later I caught Sir Robert's eye on me, and again I felt sure he said: 'I told you it would be all right. Besides, the fifth generation of the family after me is already grown up.'

The bronze statue of Monty by the distinguished sculptor the late Oscar Nemon.

This statue was erected on the lawn in Whitehall outside the Ministry of Defence main building. It was unveiled by HM The Queen Mother on 6 June 1980, the 36th anniversary of the landings on the beaches of Normandy, when Monty commanded all the Allied Land Forces under Eisenhower, in the greatest sea and airborne invasion of all time. It is not, perhaps, generally known that it was Sir Denis Hamilton who was mainly responsible for obtaining all the official, legal, financial and administrative approval, without which no statue can be erected in Whitehall.

MONTY
FIELD MARSHAL
VISCOUNT MONTGOMERY
OF ALAMEIN
1887   KG GCB DSO   1976

Finale. How it all ended. David Montgomery, the British Field
Marshall's son, together with Manfred Rommel, the German
Field Marshall's son, as they stood together jointly taking the
salute of the Eighth Army Veterans March-Past at the October
1984 Alamein Reunion.

INDEX